BEST OF

Buenos Aires

Danny Palmerlee

How to use this book

Color-Coding & Maps

Each chapter has a color code along the banner at the top of the page which is also used for text and symbols on maps (eg all venues reviewed in the Highlights chapter are orange on the maps). The fold-out maps inside the front and back covers are numbered from 1 to 7. All sights and venues in the text have map references; eg (3, C3) means Map 3, grid reference C3. See p96 for map symbols.

Prices

Multiple prices listed with reviews (eg US$10/5) usually indicate adult/concession admission to a venue. Concession prices can include senior, student, member or coupon concessions. Meal cost and room rate categories are listed at the start of the Eating and Sleeping chapters, respectively.

Text Symbols

☎ telephone
✉ address
🖳 email/website address
$ admission
☉ opening hours
ⓘ information
Ⓢ Subte
🚌 bus
🚆 train
♿ wheelchair access
🏊 swimming pool
✕ on site/nearby eatery
👶 child-friendly venue
Ⓥ good vegetarian selection
✕ nonsmoking section

Best of Buenos Aires
1st edition – Jan 2006

Published by Lonely Planet Publications Pty Ltd
ABN 36 005 607 983

Australia Head Office, Locked Bag 1, Footscray, Vic 3011
☎ 03 8379 8000 fax 03 8379 8111
🖳 talk2us@lonelyplanet.com.au
USA 150 Linden St, Oakland, CA 94607
☎ 510 893 8555 toll free 800 275 8555
fax 510 893 8572
🖳 info@lonelyplanet.com
UK 72–82 Rosebery Avenue, London EC1R 4RW
☎ 020 7841 9000 fax 020 7841 9001
🖳 go@lonelyplanet.co.uk

This title was commissioned in Lonely Planet's Oakland office and produced by: **Commissioning Editor** Suki Gear **Coordinating Editor** Fionnuala Twomey **Coordinating Cartographer** Kusnandar **Layout Designer** Jacqui Saunders **Editor** Margedd Heliosz **Cartographer** Diana Duggan **Managing Cartographer** Alison Lyall **Cover Designer** Pepi Bluck **Project Managers** Eoin Dunlevy & Glenn van der Knijff **Mapping Development** Paul Piaia **Desktop Publishing Support** Mark Germanchis **Thanks to** David Burnett, Sally Darmody, Brendan Dempsey, Quentin Frayne, Martin Heng, Rebecca Lalor, Celia Wood

Photographs by Lonely Planet Images and Krzysztof Dydynski except for the following: p5 John Hay, p34 Tom Smallman, p35 Michael Coyne, p36 Mark Newman. **Cover photograph** Buildings in La Boca district, Wayne Walton.

All images are copyright of the photographers unless otherwise indicated. Many of the images in this guide are available for licensing from Lonely Planet Images: www.lonelyplanetimages.com.

ISBN 1 74104 025 6

Printed through The Bookmaker International Ltd.
Printed in China

Contents

From the Publisher

AUTHOR
Danny Palmerlee

A freelance travel writer based in Buenos Aires, Danny has traveled extensively throughout Argentina. For over a decade, he bounced around Latin America, both for work and for play, before finally renting an apartment in the city he couldn't leave. Buenos Aires' combination of smoky steak houses, talkative old-timers, mismatched architecture and fairly priced red wine (he's from California) all conspired to suck him in. Danny is the coordinating author of Lonely Planet's *Argentina* and *South America on a shoestring*. He has covered South America and Mexico for the *Miami Herald*, the *Dallas Morning News*, the *San Francisco Chronicle*, the *Houston Chronicle* and other US publications.

First and foremost I thank my eternal partner in crime, Aimee Sabri. Only with her constant help, support and keep-on-rockin' attitude was this book possible. Huge hugs to Marissa Gordillo, Lucila Castro and Agustina 'Diablo' Carandoti for their help and hospitality. Sandra Bao's previous research for Lonely Planet's *Buenos Aires* city guide helped me immensely. Thanks also to Lonely Planet author Lucas Vidgen, who shacked up in BA for a stint and shared his favorite watering holes and restaurants with me. Suki Gear, once again, proves herself as the world's finest commissioning editor.

LONELY PLANET AUTHORS
Why is our travel information the best in the world? It's simple: our authors are independent, dedicated travelers. They don't research using just the Internet or phone, and they don't take freebies in exchange for positive coverage. They travel widely, to all the popular spots and off the beaten track. They personally visit thousands of hotels, restaurants, cafés, bars, galleries, palaces, museums and more – and they take pride in getting all the details right, and telling it how it is. For more, see the authors section on **www.lonelyplanet.com**.

PHOTOGRAPHER
Krzysztof Dydynski

Born and raised in Warsaw, Krzysztof discovered a passion for Latin America, which took him to Colombia for nearly five years. In search of a new incarnation he made Australia his new home, but has regularly returned to South America ever since, writing and photographing for Lonely Planet. Buenos Aires is one of his great loves, and he has been back time and again, revisiting his old secret corners and looking for new inspirations.

SEND US YOUR FEEDBACK
We love to hear from travelers – your comments keep us on our toes and help make our books better. Our well-traveled team reads every word on what you loved or loathed about this book. Although we cannot reply individually to postal submissions, we always guarantee that your feedback goes straight to the appropriate authors, in time for the next edition – and the most useful submissions are rewarded with a free book. To send us your updates – and find out about Lonely Planet events, newsletters and travel news – visit our award-winning website: **www.lonelyplanet.com/feedback**.

Note: We may edit, reproduce and incorporate your comments in Lonely Planet products such as guidebooks, websites and digital products, so let us know if you don't want your comments reproduced or your name acknowledged. For a copy of our privacy policy visit www.lonelyplanet.com/privacy.

Introducing Buenos Aires

Buenos Aires is a beast – a big, lovable, moody, schizophrenic metropolis with a captivating personality that's never short on surprises. It's beautiful and ugly, edgy but safe, old-fashioned yet wildly cutting edge and never, ever dull. Buenos Aires (or BA) will challenge you as you get to know it, and reward you immensely as you do. Porteños, as BA's residents are known, are impossibly friendly and bend over backward to help someone in need of directions. Although they'd never admit it, they're some of the most gregarious folks on the planet, bringing a passion to every aspect of their city.

With its rich Italian heritage, smoky old cafés, stately avenues and stunning French architecture, Buenos Aires is surprisingly European. Yet its cracked sidewalks, graffiti-covered walls and infectious street life are definitively Latin American. It's a mix that's hard to beat and impossible to duplicate. Buenos Aires' most fascinating feature is its barrios, the distinctive neighborhoods, each with its own character, that fire an insatiable desire to explore.

Most exciting of all is the urban renaissance underway right now. You'll find yourself constantly mumbling 'BA is where it's at!' Since the economic crisis of 2001, Buenos Aires has pulled itself together through creative willpower alone. Porteños have tapped their cultural riches, and are breathing new life into tango, food, wine, literature, music and art. Landing in the middle of this will give you a charge you'll never forget.

The art of tango

Neighborhoods

Buenos Aires sits on the mouth of the Río de la Plata, the widest river in the world. The **Microcentro** is the bustling, noisy city center, where beautiful old-world buildings tower over a mad frenzy of commercial chaos. Quick-footed businesspeople zip past protesters and around buses, while map-toting tourists navigate wide avenues in search of the **Plaza de Mayo** (p27), Buenos Aires' central plaza. From the Plaza de Mayo, the rest of BA's barrios (neighborhoods) are either within walking distance or a short ride away on public transportation.

The western boundary of the Microcentro is the mammoth 16-lane **Av 9 de Julio**, which porteños (BA residents) proudly claim is the widest street in the world. Once you make it across, you're either in **Congreso** (south of Av Corrientes) or **Tribunales** (north of Av Corrientes). The former is home to the **Palacio del Congreso** (House of Congress; p26), the latter to the federal *tribunales* (supreme courts). **Av Corrientes** itself is BA's theater district and the former epicenter of its glamorous nightlife.

South of Plaza de Mayo lies **Monserrat**, the city's oldest barrio. As you head further south on Defensa, the buildings shrink in size, the streets become cobbled and the appearance of antique stores and tango bars mark your presence in historic **San Telmo** (p18). Continue down Defensa and you'll hit **Parque Lezama** (p27) before entering the colorful (literally), working-class barrio of **La Boca** (p19).

Immediately north of the Microcentro is **Retiro**, one of Buenos Aires' wealthiest neighborhoods and home to numerous stunning 19th-century mansions and several art-nouveau and art-deco landmarks. Retiro's beautiful **Plaza San Martín** (p27) sits just uphill from the seedy area around the Retiro train and bus stations, conveniently cut off from the neighborhood by the wide Av del Libertador.

Northwest of Retiro, **Recoleta** is synonymous with money and death. This is BA's most prestigious barrio and home to its famed necropolis,

A tango orchestra at street level, San Telmo

Hound the streets of Buenos Aires' newest neighborhood – the stylishly reinvented Puerto Madero

the **Cementerio de la Recoleta** (p16). Here the dead sleep in style while the living reside in multistory mansions and luxurious old apartment buildings. **Barrio Norte** is the southern extension of Recoleta.

If there's one neighborhood everyone falls in love with, it's **Palermo**, northwest of Recoleta. The subneighborhood of **Palermo Viejo** (p14) is block after block of hip bars, groovy boutique shops and excellent restaurants. Across the broad Av del Libertador, Palermo's expansive parks draw porteños out from the city depths and into the sun. **Las Cañitas** is a superspendy pocket of Palermo (or Belgrano, depending on who you talk to) with superb restaurants and swanky bars.

Further north, **Belgrano** is another refuge for middle- and upper-class city dwellers. Except for the frantic shopping area along Av Cabildo (Belgrano's main artery), it's a sleepy neighborhood. Within Belgrano, **Barrio Chino** (China Town) is an interesting four-block strip along Arribeños, just north of **Barrancas de Belgrano** park (p26).

West of the center, the barrios of **Once**, **Abasto**, **Almagro** and **Caballito** are far more true to how most porteños live. Home to sizable Jewish, Korean and Peruvian populations, Once (officially known as Balvanera) is BA's most ethnically diverse barrio. *Cumbia* music blasts from its stores in aural reflection of the visual barrage of fabrics, clothes and housewares.

Directly east of the Microcentro, before you fall into the big brown Río de la Plata, is the city's newest barrio, **Puerto Madero** (p20), quickly becoming defined by luxury hotels and exclusive apartment blocks.

OFF THE BEATEN TRACK

To ditch your fellow tourists, pinball your way through Once, where they're as rare as name brands, or hit the crafts fair in **Parque Centenario** (p27). Wander the bootleg media stalls in **Parque Rivadavia** (p43), or head out to Belgrano's **China Town** for a bowl of noodle soup. In Almagro, **Las Violetas** (p59) is one of BA's most beautiful and historic cafés, and you might well be the only foreigner there.

Itineraries

Buenos Aires' wealth of museums, architecture, parks and plazas is only the surface of a city that bares its soul on its streets. Only by pounding the pavement between the main attractions will you unearth the real Buenos Aires: the newsstands, bookstores, candy kiosks, cafés, shoe-shine stands, odd specialty shops, plazas, street performers, roaming knife sharpeners, boutiques, fruit stalls and everything else you might imagine.

A Walk in the 'Hoods

Hit the **La Boca** (p19) barrio and then wander around cobblestoned **San Telmo** (p18). Have coffee at **La Puerto Rico** (p59) en route to **Plaza de Mayo** (p27). Hoof it up pedestrianized Florida to **Plaza San Martín** (p27). Still alive? Then head for the dead: **Cementerio de la Recoleta** (p16). Have a postnecropolis cocktail at **La Biela** (p59) and close the night on your feet dancing tango at **Salon Canning** (p66) in Palermo Viejo.

Ah, Palermo

Set off early and follow the **'Into the Gardens' walking tour** (p34). Then take a look through the **Museo de Arte Latinoamericano de Buenos Aires** (Malba; p21) and the **Museo Nacional de Arte Decorativo** (p23). Head to

BA independence honored by the Pirámide de Mayo, Plaza de Mayo

Palermo Viejo (p14) for some shop, shop, shopping! Have dinner at **La Cabrera** (p54) and saunter over to Plaza Serrano to send off the night.

Thou Art in Buenos Aires

Begin your modern art intake at **Malba** (p21) and then browse the **Museo Nacional de Bellas Artes** (p23). Eyeball the free exhibits at **Centro Cultural Recoleta** (p24) before hitting the outstanding **Museo Xul Solar** (p23). Dine at deliciously artful **Lomo** (p54). Day two, take in the **Centro Cultural Borges** (p24), the **Museo de Arte Moderno** (p21) and the **Museo Nacional de Arte Decorativo** (p23). Reserve a table at quirky **Sonoridad Amarilla** (p30), and close the night at the majestic **Milión** (p61).

Highlights

FÚTBOL (SOCCER)

Before you even get on the plane, pick a team. *Fútbol* is Argentina's greatest passion, and joining a stadium full of fans for a few hours of jumping, screaming, singing, arm-waving, booing and – altogether now – *¡Olé!*-ing is an unforgettable experience. On big game days, nearly all of Buenos Aires is glued to the TV set, and no matter where you are you can hear the cheers when a goal is scored. When the national team wins an important match, thousands flock to the Obelisco (p29) in joyous celebration.

Buenos Aires boasts the highest density of first-division soccer teams in the world with eight of the country's 20 teams based in the capital and another five in the suburbs. The national team won the World Cup in 1978 and 1986, and it beat Paraguay for a gold medal at the 2004 Olympics. The country's revered (and fallen) soccer hero, **Diego Maradona**, is widely considered the most gifted player ever to have graced the pitch, eclipsing even Pelé himself.

> ### HAND OF GOD
> In 1986, Buenos Aires' beloved Diego Maradona led Argentina to a World Cup victory almost single-handedly. In the semifinal that knocked England out of the tournament, he scored the two most famous goals in soccer history. In the first, he blatantly punched in a handball that referees failed to call. In the second, he dribbled past five dumbfounded outfielders *and* the goalie, winning both the game and the FIFA title of Goal of the Century. When reporters later asked him about the handball, Maradona claimed it was 'the hand of God.'

The country's two most famous teams are Buenos Aires–based **Boca Juniors** and **River Plate**. Seeing them play the *'superclásico'* match at Boca's **La Bombonera stadium** (p68) chalks in as an experience of a lifetime. The other great match is Argentina versus Brasil in River Plate's **Estadio Monumental** (p68). Barring these, any match at either stadium is something you'll never forget.

Look the part at a must-see soccer match

TANGO

Sensual, moody, erotic and serious – nothing symbolizes Buenos Aires like tango, and no visit is complete without it. In fact, a visit to BA without tango is probably impossible.

During its infancy in the city's poor *arrabales* (the working-class neighborhoods), tango was despised by the porteño (BA resident) elite, who considered it a vulgar pastime of the underclass. The earliest dance steps were created in the city's brothels by poor European immigrants who, arriving alone and en masse at the end of the 19th century, had left their loves and family behind. Men danced with men to an emerging sound that was rooted in Spanish and Italian melodies, criollo verse and Afro-Uruguayan *candombe* (a drum-based rhythm). They created theatrical, stylized movements while waiting for their turn to slip behind the bedroom door. It was a strong blend of machismo, passion and longing, with an almost fighting edge to it, symbolic of the struggle for the possession of a woman.

> ### MILONGAS
> Countless restaurants put on extravagant nightly dinner shows for tourists – 'tango for export,' as the locals call it. But if you want something a little more rootsy, hit a *milonga* (tango dance hall), where locals of all ages go to dance, *not* to perform. It is here you will see, if you watch carefully, the intricate rules and rituals of real tango: a man scanning the dance hall for a potential partner; his *cabezaso,* a quick tilt of his head signaling to a woman he wants to dance; her nod, if she's game. He escorts her to the floor and always they wait out the first few bars. Then they dance.
> See p65 for details of Buenos Aires' *milongas.*

When musicians took tango to Paris at the beginning of the 20th century, it became a craze almost overnight and soon swept through the ballrooms of Europe. By 1913, everyone wanted to dance the tango. Only then did the porteño elite allow it into their dance halls, albeit in a reserved form.

High-class tango, born from working-class passions

Tango was primarily instrumental until 1917, when a young folksinger named Carlos Gardel recorded the poetic *Mi noche triste* (My Sad Night). Considered the genre's first *tango canción* (tango song), it changed tango forever. Gardel's crooning voice and knockout charisma, and his lamenting songs of lost love, faraway mothers and changing neighborhoods, would become the musical expression of the porteño psyche.

The genre transformed over the decades with the introduction (and later decline) of orchestras; with Astor Piazzolla (who moved tango away from the dance halls toward jazz and classical); and with time.

> **DON'T MISS**
> • Wild, underground tango venue La Catedral (p66)
> • *Milonga* at Centro Cultural Torquato Tasso (p66)
> • Musical performance at Club del Vino (p61)
> • Dinner show at Bar Sur (p65)
> • Tango lesson and *milonga* at Salon Canning (p66)

Less than a decade ago, most porteños considered tango a nostalgic hobby for old-timers and tourists. But after the economic crisis in 2000, something changed. Whether tango's mournful lament found newly sympathetic ears or the explosion of tango-hungry tourists jacked up demand, tango bounced back – big time. Classes filled up, exrocker Daniel Melingo turned out hard-edge tangos with contemporary lyrics, and music collectives Bajofondo Tango Club and Paris-based Gotan Project ignited an entirely new tango *electrónica* subgenre. Despite its nap for a few decades, the tango scene in Buenos Aires is now so vibrant it can be overwhelming.

See p65 for details on where you can see, hear and – if you're daring – dance tango.

There's always a time and a place for tango

BEEF

Start off with a bit of blood sausage, followed by crisply grilled intestines with a squeeze of lemon, half a beef sausage, a little kidney and finally some tender sweetbreads (thymus gland). Continue with a slab of short ribs, a couple of slices of flank steak and a little sirloin to finish things off. Out walks the grill man, and a *gran aplauso* (big applause) all around.

So goes the typical Argentine *asado* (barbecue), when family and friends gather on weekends for some good, old fashioned meat-eating fun. Of course, not everyone in Buenos Aires has a grill (or the hours required to buy and cook everything), which is where the ubiquitous *parrilla* (grill restaurant) comes in. Here, the mighty mix of meats is delivered on a tabletop grill allowing the diner to pick, poke and continue cooking the meats to their liking. The *parrilla* is also the place where the visitor to Buenos Aires can get in on the action.

But what's all the fuss? Why is Argentine beef so special? Ask any porteño, and with sweeping arms they'll imitate the vast, fertile grasslands of the Pampas, Argentina's agricultural heartland, explaining that, with grass so thick, a cow never has to move. It just stands there, head in the ruff, getting fatter and softer than its bovine cousins elsewhere. And because Argentine cows fatten up on nutritious Pampas grass (and more recently barley and alfalfa), rather than corn-feed and growth hormones, they produce a leaner, more natural-tasting beef.

For centuries, Argentine ranchers have kept strict control over breeding, crossing European with mostly British stock to create the highest quality (and to this day, mostly free-range) beef. The *asado* originated with Argentina's gauchos, the nomadic horsemen who worked the cattle herds for large *estancias* (traditional grazing estates) and slaughtered cows to cook on the spot over an open spit. To this day, Argentine beef is not aged as in the US or Britain, giving it a distinct flavor.

A sizzle of barbecued chorizos

A side order of salad, anyone?

On your first venture to a *parrilla,* getting what you want, exactly how you want it, is not a simple task. If you're not keen on *achuras* (organ meats), steer clear of the *parrillada* (mixed grill). *Parrillada* is usually intended to share between two or more people, and it almost invariably includes delicacies like *chinchulines* (intestines), *morcilla* (blood sausage), chorizo (sausage), and less expensive, often chewier cuts of meat like *asado de tira* (a narrow strip of short ribs), *vacío* (flank steak) and *chuleta* (chop). The *parrillada* is a real treat, however, and one to experience at least once.

The tactic for moving straight to the choice cuts is to order items separately. Argentina's definitive steak is the *bife de chorizo* (sirloin; not to be confused with the sausage chorizo). Other cuts not to be missed include *bife de lomo* (tenderloin), the succulent *ojo de bife* (rib eye) and *entrecot* (entrecôte) or *bife ancho* (a boneless rib cut). Another delicious cut, often available as *cerdo* (pork), is *matambre,* a thinly sliced cut from between the ribs and hide. *Churrasco* is also a thin steak, which was a favorite among the gauchos, who needed a quick-cooking piece of meat to eat between shifts on the range. *Cuadril* is rump steak.

Argentines tend to like their meat *cocido* (well done), which, for most foreigners, is equivalent to well charred. For medium, order your steak *a punto* and for rare ask for *jugoso.* For extra flavor, dash on some *chimichurri* (oil and herb sauce), and you're good to go.

DON'T MISS
- La Cabrera (p54)
- La Dorita (p54)
- El Portugués (p55)
- La Brigada (p51)

Grilled beef – the backbone of every *parrilla*

PALERMO VIEJO (7, B4)

Home to the city's hippest restaurants, coolest cafés, trendiest bars and hottest designers, this subdivision of BA's biggest barrio, Palermo, is captivating in every sense. Further divided into **Palermo Soho** and **Palermo Hollywood**, its leafy streets make it easy to forget the rest of Buenos Aires exists.

Take yourself straight to the heart of cool by heading to the neighborhood's focal point: the small **Plaza Serrano** (7, B5; officially Plaza Julio Cortázar). Flanked by cafés and bars with outdoor tables, this is where folks break from their shopping spree to sip *cortados* (coffee cut with milk) in the sunshine. By night, the plaza transforms into an outdoor party, where revelers gather outside the bars to chat beneath the trees. On sunny weekends, the plaza takes on a different hue: select local artists display and sell their paintings at the **Feria de Arte Palermo Viejo** (p43).

Radiating outward from Plaza Serrano, tree-lined streets harbor fabulous boutique shops in old, two-story buildings and stylishly converted lofts. Around every corner lies surprises, from funky little soap and paper shops, to eye-popping outlets like **Juana de Arco** (p40), **Calma Chicha** (p39) and design guru Ingrid Gutman's **Humawaca** (p40). With more than 200 clothing and accessory shops and over 100 design and furniture stores, covering Palermo Viejo in a day is impossible. To see what's out there and where, pick up a couple of the free categorized maps that pinpoint nearly every business in Palermo.

INFORMATION

- ✉ loosely, the area bound by Avs Córdoba, Dorrego, Santa Fe and Scalabrini Ortiz
- ☿ most shops close on Sunday
- ⓘ excellent maps available free at most stores and cafés
- ▣ 55 & 166 to Plaza Serrano (Plaza Cortázar); otherwise, any bus to Plaza Italia
- Ⓜ Line D, Plaza Italia
- ♿ good, but a few curb ramps
- ✖ p53

Take a break from shopping in one of Palermo Viejo's shaded cafés

DON'T MISS

- Plaza Serrano on a weekend night
- Mercado de Pulgas (Flea Market; p29)
- Shopping around the intersection of El Salvador and Armenia (7, B5)

FERIA DE MATADEROS

Every weekend, hordes of porteños and a smattering of tourists leave the concrete canyons of central Buenos Aires and descend upon the western suburb of Mataderos for an authentic celebration of Argentine country life, folk music and gaucho traditions. If you're in town on a weekend, it's not to be missed.

Named for the slaughterhouses that once filled the neighborhood, Mataderos is no longer the butcher block it once was, but it is still home to the **Mercado Nacional de Hacienda**, a major livestock market. On Sundays the market fills not with livestock but with craft vendors, food stalls and musicians. Argentine folk music (rather than tango) spills from the outdoor stage, and people take to the street and dance the *chacarera,* the *chamamé* and the *samba.* Food stalls dish out traditional delicacies like *locro* (a hearty stew from northwest Argentina), empanadas, *humitas* (lightly sweetened corn meal wrapped in corn husks) and, of course, plenty of *choripanes* (sausage sandwiches). The old market building now houses the interesting **Museo Criollo de los Corrales** (☎ 4687-1949; admission US$0.35; ⏰ noon-6pm Sun & holidays), with displays of old gaucho implements, leather work, horse-drawn carts and a small replica of a traditional *pulpería* (saloon).

Beginning around 3:30pm, the most exciting event of all takes place: the *sortija.* In handsome gaucho regalia, horsemen ride full speed down the street – standing up and with eyes wide as saucers – and attempt to spear a tiny ring dangling from a ribbon.

INFORMATION

- ☎ 4374-9664 Mon-Fri, 4687-5602 Sun
- 🖳 www.feriademataderos.com.ar in Spanish
- ✉ cnr Lisandro de la Torre & Av de los Corrales, Mataderos
- 💲 free
- ⏰ 11am-6pm Sun, Apr-Dec; 6pm-1am Sat, Jan-Mar
- 🚌 55, 92, 126, 180 (R155)
- ♿ good, flat, but often crowded
- 🍴 food stalls

Fun and games during the Feria de Mataderos

A BLOODY WINDY CITY

Mataderos was once home to the city's slaughterhouses and was nicknamed Nueva Chicago (New Chicago) for the cattle butchering it had in common with the Windy City of yore. 'Nueva Chicago' signs, such as the one at the entrance to Parque Dr Juan Alberdi, still adorn the neighborhood, but the slaughterhouses are a thing of the past.

CEMENTERIO DE LA RECOLETA (2, B1)

As the saying goes, it's cheaper to live extravagantly your entire life than to be buried in Recoleta. Indeed, securing a burial site in the Cementerio de la Recoleta, one of the world's greatest necropolises, is close to impossible.

INFORMATION

☎ 4804-7040, 4803-1594
✉ Junín 1790, Recoleta
$ free
⏱ 7am-6pm
ℹ free tours in English 11am Tue & Thu, weather permitting
🚌 17, 29, 61, 62, 67, 92, 93, 110
♿ excellent
✖ Florencio (p52)

The living celebrate the dead at Recoleta cemetery, burial place of Eva Perón

Even the embalmed body of **Evita Perón** had to be snuck in under the cover of darkness in 1974, more than 20 years after her death. For the living, however, entry is free.

Although the tourist information kiosk (⏱ 8am–6pm) outside the main entrance provides a handy map (US$1.50) of the burial sites of politicians, writers and artists, the greatest pleasure is wandering aimlessly through the mazelike necropolis. It's truly a city in miniature, with masterful art-deco, art-nouveau, neoclassical neo-Gothic, Byzantine and Greek tombs, some crumbling and cobwebbed, adding to the sense of macabre. Occasionally you can peak through a broken window and see the ornate, dusty coffins stacked as deep as the eye can see in the tradition of Recoleta burials. Feral cats wander the alleyways giving the entire scene a Gotham-like feel, especially on cloudy days.

Among marble angels and black granite tombs you'll find the sites of some of Argentina's most famous – and infamous – historical figures: 19th-century educator and president **Domingo Sarmiento**, *caudillo* (strongman) **Juan Facundo Quiroga** (occupying the cemetery's oldest tomb), politician **Carlos de Alvear**, Radical party leader **Leandro Além**, twice-president **Hipólito Yrigoyen**, boxing great **Angel Firpo**, independence hero **William Brown** and writer **Victoria Ocampos**.

CHACARITA: THE OTHER CEMETERY

And what about tango legend Carlos Gardel? Former president Juan Perón? Aviator Jorge Newberry? Funny you should ask. They, along with many other popular Argentine heroes, are buried in **Cementerio Chacarita** (3, B2; cnr Avs Federico Lacroze & Guzman; ⏱ 7am-6pm), Argentina's largest cemetery. Opened in the 1870s to accommodate the yellow-fever victims of San Telmo and La Boca, the more egalitarian cemetery of La Chacarita is fascinating to see, especially the tomb of Carlos Gardel, the most visited grave in the country.

TEATRO COLÓN (4, D1)

Snuggling into a red-velvet seat for an opera at the Teatro Colón is undeniably one of Buenos Aires' most magical experiences. Inaugurated in 1908 with a performance of Verdi's *Aída*, the Teatro Colón easily falls into the world's top-five list of opera houses. As impressive as its beauty are its acoustics, which some experts deem the best in the world.

The Colón's seven tiers rise in a magnificent horseshoe shape around the stage and seat 4748 people, with room for another 500 standing in the 'chicken coup' up top. The main chandelier, lit by over 700 bulbs, hangs within a 318-sq-meter cupola, covered in murals by Argentine painter Raúl Soldi. The opulent entry hall is dominated by the grand 'Stairway of Honor,' made of Verona and Carrara marble and anchored by two giant marble lions. Above, busts of famous composers adorn the Salon de los Bustos.

Although opera season officially runs March through December, there are choral, orchestral and ballet performances year-round,

INFORMATION

- ☎ 4378-7344, tour reservations 4378-7132/7133
- ✉ Libertad 621; tours depart from Tucumán 1171
- $ performances US$2-75; tours US$4
- ⏰ performance times vary; tours in Spanish 11am, noon, 1pm, 2:30pm, 3pm & 4pm Mon-Sat, 11am, noon, 1pm, 2pm, & 3pm Sun; tours in English 11am, 1pm & 3pm daily
- ℹ reserve tours at least one day in advance
- 🚌 23, 29, 39, 75, 99, 102, 115, 140
- Ⓜ Line D, Tribunales
- ♿ difficult

A HISTORY TO SING ABOUT

The Teatro Colón was the largest theater in the southern hemisphere until the construction of the Sydney Opera House in 1973. It remains South America's most important classical music venue. Since its inauguration it has hosted some of the world's greatest performers, including composers Richard Strauss and Igor Stravinsky, dancers Anna Pavlova, Rudolf Nureyev, Mikhail Barishnikov and Vaslav Nijinsky, conductors Arturo Toscanini and Herbert von Karajan, and singers Enrico Caruso, Plácido Domingo and Luciano Pavarotti. And that's only to name a few.

including works by the excellent Buenos Aires Philharmonic Orchestra. If you can't make a show (and even if you can), take one of the fascinating tours that guide you through the halls and into the labyrinthine basement workshops, where everything – from the sets to the costumes and jewelry – is made onsite. You'll even get to sit in the presidential box.

SAN TELMO (5, B2)

With its cobblestone streets, low-story colonial architecture, tiny cafés, and backstreet bohemian flair, San Telmo is the city's most atmospheric barrio. **Plaza Dorrego** (5, C2) is the heart of the neighborhood and home to the **Feria de San Telmo** (🕙 10am-5pm Sat & Sun) antiques fair. Every Sunday, the streets surrounding the plaza are blocked off to cars, and tourists and locals pour in to browse the antiques and watch tango in the streets and in many of the surrounding restaurants. The Saturday version is smaller.

The main artery into San Telmo is Defensa, named for the violent street fighting that took place when British troops, at war with Spain, invaded the city in 1806 and 1807. When the British forces advanced up the street, an impromptu militia poured cauldrons of boiling oil and water from the rooftops, driving them back to their ships. After a yellow-fever epidemic hit the once-fashionable San Telmo area in the late 19th century, the porteño elite evacuated to higher ground in and around current-day Recoleta. As European immigrants poured into the city, former mansions were turned into *conventillos* (tenements), housing poor families in wretchedly cramped quarters. For a peek inside one of these, visit **Pasaje de la Defensa** (5, C2; Defensa 1179), now charmingly chaotic with antiques stores.

> **DON'T MISS**
> • Casa Mínima (5, C1), a 2m-wide house, the narrowest abode in the city
> • Parque Lezama (p27)
> • Museo de Arte Moderno (p21)
> • Weekday coffee at Plaza Dorrego tables

People-watching in San Telmo

> **INFORMATION**
> ✉ loosely, the area bound by Av Chile, Av 9 de Julio, Paseo Colón & Parque Lezama
> 🚌 10, 20, 29, 74, 86 & others, all to Plaza Dorrego
> Ⓜ Line C, Independencia or San Juan
> ♿ Plaza Dorrego limited during feria; best on Sunday when streets closed to traffic
> 🍴 p50

LA BOCA (5, D3)

Truth be told, **El Caminito** (5, D6) – La Boca's famous alleyway of multi-colored wood and corrugated-tin houses – is about as touristy as it gets. But no matter how many camera clickers stomp through, La Boca never loses its magical, roughed-up appeal.

Named for its location on the *boca* (mouth) of the Riachuelo river, La Boca was the city's principal port until Puerto Madero was built at the close of the 19th century. The neighborhood owes its colorful history to the thousands of Italian immigrants who settled here in the late 1900s, and painted their houses with cans of colorful paint they bummed from the harbored ships. They unwittingly created the patchwork of colors that made La Boca famous.

El Caminito, the Little Walkway, is a short, curved alleyway named after a 1926 tango song and forms the tourist core of an otherwise rough-and-tumble neighborhood. Although today tango is associated more with San Telmo, it was invented in the brothels and cantinas of La Boca. The marvelous little **Café La Perla** (☎ 4301-2985; Av Don Pedro de Mendoza 1899; ☯ 8am-9pm), a former brothel, offers a glimpse into that sultry past.

South of Parque Lezama, a giant, colorful **frieze** (5, C3) marks the entrance to the barrio, and a sign reads 'La Republica de la Boca.' Indeed, La Boca remains a hardened, self-determined, working-class neighborhood whose denizens identify far more passionately with their soccer club – the legendary Club Atlético Boca Juniors – than with just about anything else in Buenos Aires.

INFORMATION

- ✉ neighborhood boundaries: Avs Martín García, Patricios and Brasil, and the Riachuelo river
- ☯ best in the morning for photographic light and before tourist buses arrive; don't wander after dark
- ⓘ El Caminito is packed on weekends. Venturing away from the streets immediately around El Caminito and the area between El Caminito and La Bombonera is not advised.
- 🚌 20, 25, 29, 33, 53, 64, 152
- ♿ good, but a few curb ramps
- ✖ El Obrero (p51)

The irresistibly colorful El Caminito, La Boca

DON'T MISS

- Museo de la Pasión Boquense (p22)
- Fundación Proa (p21)
- Restaurant and blues club **El Samovar de Rasputín** (☎ 4302-3190; Del Valle Iberlucea 1251)
- Soccer match at La Bombonera stadium (p68)

PUERTO MADERO & COSTANERA SUR (3, E2)

At the renovated docklands of Puerto Madero, upscale restaurants occupy converted red-brick warehouses and private yachts float restfully in the port's four sun-baked *diques* (harbor basins). Puerto Madero's signature monument is the striking **Puente de la Mujer** (4, J4); resembling something between a sundial and a fishhook, the bridge actually represents a couple dancing the tango.

INFORMATION

✉ area east of Microcentro & San Telmo
🚌 20, 74, 64, 129, 152 & others
🚇 Line A, Plaza de Mayo; Line D, Catedral; Line E, Bolivar; Line B LN Alem
♿ excellent
✗ p48 and cheap *parrillas* (grill restaurants) on ER de Dellepiane, Costanera Sur

Built in the 1890s, Puerto Madero proved quickly inadequate for Buenos Aires' increasing trade and was abandoned less than two decades after its completion. It reopened to the public in 1994, and developers quickly brought in chain hotels and restaurants. Despite Puerto Madero's exclusivity, there's plenty to see, including the **Museo Fragata Sarmiento** (4, J4; ☎ 4334-9386; Dique 3; admission US$0.75; ⏲ 9am-6pm), a naval ship turned museum, and the educational **Museo de la Inmigración** (6, F1; ☎ 4317-0285; Av Antártida Argentina 1355; admission free; ⏲ 10am-5pm Mon-Fri, 11am-6pm Sat & Sun).

Due east of the port lies the far more down-to-earth Costanera Sur, a wide, tree-lined promenade skirting the city's largest open space, the **Reserva Ecológica Costanera Sur** (3, E2; ⏲ 8am-7pm Nov-Mar, 8am-6pm Apr-Oct, closed Mon), excellent for bird-watching. The promenade, built between 1916 and 1918, was once the city's beloved **balneario municipal** (3, E2; public swimming site), until landfill pushed the Río de la Plata east. The prettiest sights of all are the **waterfront pillars** (3, E2) at Azucena Villaflor and the nearby **Fuente de las Nereidas** (5, E1; Av TA Rodríguez & Padre Migone), a beautiful marble fountain created in 1903 by Tucumán artist Lola Mora. The promenade is also known for the colorful, makeshift **barbecue carts** that sell delicious steak sandwiches to afternoon strollers.

WHERE THE STREETS HAVE HER NAME

In contrast to the men's names given to practically every street in Buenos Aires, nearly all the streets in Puerto Madero are named after women. Included are socialist and feminist Alicia Moreau de Justo (1885–1986), women's education activist Mariquita Sánchez de Thompson (1786–1868) and writer Victoria Ocampo (1890–1979). Puerto Madero's famous bridge is dedicated to women, and one of the city's most famous sculptures, Fuente de las Nereidas, was designed by Tucumán artist Lola Mora in 1903.

Sights & Activities

MUSEUMS

Fundación Proa (5, E6)
While most of the waterfront area around La Boca's El Caminito panders to tourists, this outstanding art foundation and museum is an exception. Cutting-edge national and international artists are invited to show here, with results well worth the minimal entry fee.
☎ 4303-0909 🖳 www.proa .org in Spanish ✉ Av Don Pedro de Mendoza 1929 💲 US$1 🕑 11am-7pm Tue-Sun 🚌 29, 64 ♿ good

Museo Casa Carlos Gardel (3, D2)
Occupying the former home of tango legend Carlos Gardel (he moved here when he was 37), this small museum traces the singer's career through a small display of records, sheet music, photos and artwork. Perhaps even more interesting is the colorful *filete* paintings on the buildings outside (for more on *filete*, see the boxed text, p22).
☎ 4964-2015/2071 ✉ Jean Jaurés 735, Abasto 💲 US$1

🕑 11am-6pm Mon & Wed-Fri, 10am-7pm Sat & Sun 🚇 Line B, Pueyrredón ♿ fair

Museo de Arte Latinoamericano de Buenos Aires (Malba) (7, F3)
If there's one art museum you don't want to miss, Malba is it. Opened in 2001 and housing the private collection of Argentine multimillionaire Eduardo Costantini, Malba is home to exceptional works by Latin American greats, including Frida Kahlo and Diego Rivera, and Argentines Antonio Berni, Xul Solar and Emilio Pettoruti. Temporary exhibits are nearly always exceptional as well.
☎ 4808-6500 🖳 www .malba.org.ar ✉ Av Presidente Figueroa Alcorta 3415, Palermo 💲 US$2 🕑 noon-9pm Wed, noon-8pm Thu-Mon 🚌 17, 124, 130 ♿ excellent

Museo de Arte Moderno (5, C2)
Housed in a recycled tobacco warehouse, this excellent, small and underappreciated

Remember to look up at Malba

modern art museum show-cases some of Argentina's best contemporary artists.
☎ 4361-1121 ✉ Av San Juan 350, San Telmo 💲 US$1, free Wed 🕑 10am-8pm Tue-Fri, 11am-8pm Sat & Sun 🚌 10, 20, 22, 29, 86 ♿ good

Museo de Artes Plásticas Eduardo Sívori (7, D1)
This beautifully located modern art museum displays paintings and sculptures of more than 100 of the country's most established artists. It's quite a range of work, both in quality and

STREETWISE

Av 9 de Julio Wide? Nah, c'mon it's not *that* wide. What's 16 lanes?
Av Alvear Recoleta's grandest avenue; don't confuse with Av MT de Alvear.
Av Corrientes Theaters, bookstores and pizza galore.
Av de Mayo BA's most historic avenue; beautiful buildings and famous cafés; don't confuse with Av 25 de Mayo.
Av del Libertador Main artery into the city, bedecked with giant monuments.
Av Pueyrredón Heart of Once; wholesale, low-budget consumer mayhem near the intersection of Av Rivadavia.
Av Santa Fe Shop till you drop from foot to top.
Defensa Main drag into San Telmo; antiques galore.
Florida Pedestrian heart of Retiro; high-end shopping, leather, leather, leather.
Lavalle Pedestrian cinema stretch between Av 9 de Julio and San Martín; carnival-like fun on weekend nights.

quantity, and well worth a visit before a saunter through the nearby Rosedal (p27).
☎ 4774-9452 ⌨ www
.museosivori.org.ar in Spanish
✉ Av de la Infanta Isabel 555, Palermo 💲 US$0.35
🕑 noon-6pm Tue-Fri, 10am-6pm Sat & Sun, until 8pm Dec-Jun 🚌 10, 34 ♿ good

Museo de Bellas Artes de La Boca (5, E6)

Argentine painter Benito Quinquela Martín (1890–1977) lived and worked in this building, now a museum housing an outstanding collection of his haunting paintings of the ships and dockworkers of La Boca's past.
☎ 4301-1080 ✉ Av Don Pedro de Mendoza 1835, La Boca 💲 US$0.35
🕑 10am-5:30pm Tue-Fri, 11am-5:30pm Sat & Sun
🚌 29, 64 ♿ excellent

Museo de la Ciudad (4, G4)

Through historical photographs, old furniture, salvaged doors, building motifs and even toys and hardware, the Museum of the City conjures an image of old Buenos Aires.
☎ 4331-9855 ✉ Adolfo Alsina 412, Monserrat
💲 US$1, free Wed
🕑 11am-7pm Mon-Fri, 3-7pm Sat & Sun 🚇 Line A, Plaza de Mayo; Line E, Bolívar

Museo de la Pasión Boquense (5, D6)

No visit to La Boca is complete without stopping into this futuristic shrine to the Club Atlético Boca Juniors soccer club. Step inside a giant soccer ball, where a 360-degree movie screen will transport you into a crowd-filled stadium. Other exhibits highlight everything from famous goals to player stats.
☎ 4362-1100 ⌨ www
.museoboquense.com in Spanish ✉ Brandsen 805
💲 adult/child under 12 US$2.75/1.35 🕑 10am-7pm
🚌 29, 64 ♿ good

Museo Evita (7, D3)

Whether saint or tyrant (a question posed by the museum's first display), this is all about adoration for Eva (Evita) Perón. It's a highly educational walking tour through her life, with touches like video montages set to tango *electrónica* – a nice break after admiring all her fabulous gowns. Information is available in English.
☎ 4807-9433 ✉ Lafinur 2988, Palermo 💲 US$1.70
🕑 3-8pm Tue-Sun 🚌 15, 59, 60, 64, 93 & others
♿ good

Museo Histórico Nacional (5, C3)

Supposedly this is the exact site where Pedro de Mendoza founded the city in 1536. True or not, the museum is an interesting tribute to BA's past, with paintings of Mendoza's expeditions, Jesuit settlements, the British invasions of 1806 and 1807, the struggle for independence from Spain and portraits of national heroes. Lots of knickknacks, weapons and artifacts too.

FILETE PORTEÑO

It's said that while tango is an expression of sadness, *filete* – Buenos Aires' other folk art – is a celebration. Walk around San Telmo and you'll see the finely painted linework, curlicues and flowers of *filete*, a decorative painting style that emerged at the end of the 19th century as a form of distinguishing horse-drawn carts. The style moved to trucks and later to public buses, until the military government of 1976–83 outlawed *filete* on public transport. Today, several *fileteadores* (painters) sell works to tourists at craft markets. Also check out the new and beautiful *filete* buildings along Jean Jaurés, outside the Museo Casa Carlos Gardel (p21).

Now *that's* a facade

☎ 4307-1182 ⊠ Defensa 1600, San Telmo $ US$0.75 🕑 11am-5pm Tue-Fri, 11am-7pm Sun 🚌 29, 39, 53, 64 & others 🚻 limited due to stairs

Museo Municipal de Arte Hispanoamericano Isaac Fernández Blanco (6, C1)

Housed in the Palacio Noel, a neocolonial mansion built in 1921, this interesting museum features an exceptional collection of colonial art including silverwork from Alto Perú (present-day Bolivia), religious paintings, Jesuit statuary, costumes, furniture, colonial silverware and antiques.

☎ 4327-0228 ⊠ Suipacha 1422, Retiro $ US$1 🕑 2-7pm Tue-Sun 🚌 17, 59, 61, 93, 152 🚻 staff will help with stairs

Museo Nacional de Arte Decorativo (7, F4)

Housed in the stunning beaux-arts mansion Palacio Errázuriz (1911–17), this museum begs one question: someone *lived* here?! Yes, indeed. Chilean aristocrat Matías Errázuriz and his wife, Josefina de Alvear did, and some 4000 of their very posh belongings – from Louis XIV furniture to Renaissance religious paintings to Italian

sculptures – are on show for your enjoyment. Don't miss it.
☎ 4806-8306 🖳 www .mnad.org ⊠ Av del Libertador 1902, Palermo $ US$0.70, free Tue 🕑 2-7pm Tue-Sun 🚌 21, 38, 59, 60, 118 & others 🚻 good

Museo Nacional de Bellas Artes (2, B1)

The country's most important fine-arts venue contains an impressive collection of 19th- and 20th-century Argentine art, as well as works by European masters such as Renoir, Rodin, Monet, Toulouse-Lautrec, Gauguin, Rembrandt and Van Gogh. Paintings by Argentines such as Angel Della Valle and Prilidiano Pueyrredón depict 19th-century country and gaucho life, while more modern paintings follow European art movements with Argentine themes.
☎ 4803-0802 🖳 www .aamnba.com.ar ⊠ Av del Libertador 1473, Recoleta $ free 🕑 12:30-7:30pm Tue-Fri, 9:30am-7:30pm Sat & Sun 🚌 17, 67, 92, 93, 110 🚻 limited

Museo Xul Solar (7, E6)

One of the leading (though often marginalized) figures of the Argentine avant-garde, painter and

Welcome to the Museo Nacional de Arte Decorativo

inventor Alejandro Xul Solar (1887–1963) was one interesting fellow. Along with his paintings of fantastic, imaginary worlds, the museum houses exhibits on his 'universal language,' the colored piano keyboard he created to speed up learning, and his 'pan chess' game. The museum itself is an architectural masterpiece.
☎ 4824-3302 🖳 www .xulsolar.org.ar in Spanish ⊠ Laprida 1212, Palermo $ US$1 🕑 noon-8pm Tue-Fri, noon-7pm Sat Ⓜ Line D, Agüero 🚻 limited due to stairs inside

GOING DEEPER

Anyone interested in exploring the architecture of Buenos Aires beyond the major landmark buildings should pick up a copy of *Guía de Edificios, Sitios y Paisajes,* published by the Secretary of Culture's Dirección General de Patrimonio (dgPat). Although it's in Spanish, each of the 194 historical buildings, sites and plazas is tagged with a photo and a map, making it easy to pick the ones you want to see. It's sold at the Tienda Cultural (p44) and costs US$8. For another US$6, pick up dgPat's *Guía de Murales,* detailing and mapping 163 works of public art.

CULTURAL CENTERS

In many respects, BA's *centros culturales* (cultural centers) are the backbone of the city's arts and culture scenes. Whether for their bookstores, art exhibitions, movie theaters or evening performances, all are worth a visit. There are numerous in the city; the following are the most central.

Centro Cultural Borges
(4, F1)
It may be small, but the gallery is excellent, and changing exhibits run the visual arts gamut from award-winning local photographers to Andy Warhol.
☎ 5555-5359 ☐ www .ccborges.org.ar in Spanish ✉ Galerías Pacífico, cnr Viamonte & San Martín, Retiro ⑤ free ⏱ 10am-9pm Mon-Sat, noon-9pm Sun ◉ Line B, Florida ♿ limited due to stairs

Centro Cultural Konex
(4, C1)
One of the city's most important cultural centers, Konex offers everything from cheap tango classes and musical performances to art exhibits, theater and independent films. In 2006/2007, Konex plans to open a mega cultural complex, called the Ciudad Cultural Konex, at Sarmiento 3100 in Abasto.
☎ 4816-1100 ☐ www .centroculturalkonex.org in Spanish ✉ Av Córdoba 1235, Congreso ⑤ varies ⏱ 3-8pm Mon-Fri ◉ Line D, Tribunales ♿ good

Centro Cultural Recoleta
(2, B1)
Immediately adjacent to the Cementerio de la Recoleta (p16), this is one of Buenos Aire's best cultural centers, and the excellent galleries inside showcase some of the country's most sought-after artists. The center's bookstore is one of the city's finest, plus there's a cinema and the Museo Participativo de Ciencias (p31).
☎ 4803-1041 ☐ www .centroculturalrecoleta.org in Spanish ✉ Junín 1930, Recoleta ⑤ US$0.35 ⏱ 2-9pm Tue-Fri, 10am-9pm Sat & Sun ☐ 17, 62 , 67, 93, 110 ♿ good

NOTABLE BUILDINGS & LANDMARKS

Biblioteca Nacional
(2, B1)
A massive futuristic mushroom of a building, the national library looks like it could launch into space if not for the weight of the five million books and documents inside. Built on the site where Eva and Juan Perón lived (the home was razed by the post-Perón government), the national library is a sight to behold.
☎ 4808-6088 ☐ www .bibnal.edu.ar in Spanish ✉ Agüero 2502, Recoleta ⑤ free ⏱ 9am-9pm Mon-Fri, noon-7pm Sat & Sun ☐ 21, 59, 60, 93, 110 ♿ fair

Cabildo de Buenos Aires
(4, G4)
Built in 1725, this was the original seat of government and the birthplace of the struggle toward independence from Spain. Its current arcade, built in 1940, is a restoration of the original 11 arches that stretched across the width of Plaza de Mayo until they were demolished to make room for Av de Mayo

---

BLOCK OF ENLIGHTENMENT

The **Manzana de las Luces** (Block of Enlightenment; 4, F5) was once Buenos Aires' center of learning. Jesuit missionaries built their university here in the early 1700s, educating many of the country's leading thinkers. They also built what is now the city's oldest colonial church, the Iglesia San Ignacio. On the north side of the block, two of the five original buildings of the Procuraduría (Jesuit headquarters) still stand. On the west side is the Colegio Nacional de Buenos Aires, Argentina's most esteemed secondary school. Beneath the buildings lie a series of tunnels discovered in 1912. **Tours** (admission US$1; 3pm Mon-Fri; 3pm, 4:30pm & 6pm Sat & Sun) in Spanish provide the only regular public access to the block's interior. Tickets are sold at the **Comisión Nacional de la Manzana de las Luces** (☎ 4331-9534; Perú 272).

and Av Julio Roca. Inside, the small museum offers a fine view over Plaza de Mayo.
☎ 4342-6729 ✉ Bolívar 65, Microcentro 💲 free ⏲ museum 10:30am-5pm Tue-Fri, 11:30am-6pm Sun 🚇 Line A, Perú; Line D, Catedral; Line E, Bolívar

Casa Rosada (4, H4)
This is BA's equivalent to the USA's White House, only it's pink, approachable by civilians nearly to the front door, and home to the presidential offices only, not the bedrooms (the prez sleeps in the suburb of Olivos). Inaugurated in 1898, Casa Rosada was built on the site of BA's original fort, whose ruins are visible from inside the attached Casa Rosada museum (entrance Hipólito Yrigoyen 219; admission free; ⏲ 10am-6pm Mon-Fri, 2-6pm Sun). Guided tours of the palace leave the museum at 3pm and 4:30pm Sunday.
✉ Balcarce 50, Microcentro 🚇 Line A, Plaza de Mayo; Line D, Catedral; Line E, Bolívar

Edificio Kavanagh (6, E2)
One of the capital's most prized buildings, this 120m-high art-deco landmark was the tallest concrete structure in the world when it was built

Salute the pink hues of the Casa Rosada

in 1935. It scrapes the sky across from Plaza San Martín.
✉ Florida 1035, Retiro 🚇 Line C, San Martín

Palacio Barolo (4, C4)
In 1923, Italian Mario Palanti created this architectural tribute to Dante's *Divine Comedy*. At 100m, its height matches the number of songs in the work, and with 22 floors, the number of stanzas per song. Hell is below, Purgatory is next, and Heaven's up top, where a lighthouse was built to shine as far as Montevideo's Palacio Salvo, also built by Palanti.
✉ Av de Mayo 1370, Congreso/Monserrat 🚇 Line A, Sáenz Peña

Palacio de Correos (4, H2)
Inaugurated in 1928, the enormous Palacio de Correos took over 50 years to build

and is a stunning example of the French classical style so popular in Buenos Aires (though it was inspired by New York's central post office). It's still the administrative HQ of Argentina's postal system, see p88.
☎ 4316-3000 ✉ Av Sarmiento 151, Microcentro 💲 free ⏲ 8am-8pm Mon-Fri, 9am-1pm Sat 🚇 Line B, LN Alem ♿ fair

Palacio de Justicia (4, C2)
Fronting Plaza Lavalle and occupying an entire city block, this colossal beaux-arts building was constructed in stages between 1904 and 1949. It's home to the country's *tribunales* (supreme courts).
✉ Talcahuano 550, Congreso 🚇 Line B, Uruguay; Line D, Tribunales

Palacio de las Aguas Corrientes (4, A1)
Inaugurated in 1894 and decorated with over 300,000 British terracotta tiles, this hodgepodge of architectural styles is home to the city's now privatized waterworks. The 12 giant tanks that formerly filled the building once distributed water to the city. The museum inside has an astounding collection of old urinals and toilets.

Launch yourself into the Biblioteca Nacional

☎ 6319-1104
✉ Riobamba 750,
Congreso $ free
🕐 museum 9am-1pm
Mon-Fri 🔵 Line D, Callao or
Facultad de Medicina

Palacio del Congreso
(4, A4)
A cross between Berlin's
Reichstag and the US
Capitol Building, Argentina's
national House of Congress
is an imposing work of gray
limestone topped by an 85m
green dome. It was built
between 1897 and 1906.
Free tours of the Senate in
English are given at 11am
and 4pm, 5pm and 6pm
Monday to Friday.
☎ 4010-3000 ✉ cnr Avs
Entre Ríos & Rivadavia,
Congreso $ free 🔵 Line A,
Congreso

Palacio San Martín (6, D2)
This art-nouveau mansion,
facing Plaza San Martín, was
originally built for the elite
Anchorena family but later
became the headquarters of
the Foreign Ministry.
✉ Arenales 761, Retiro
🔵 Line C, San Martín

PARKS & PLAZAS

Barrancas de Belgrano
(3, A3)
Out in Belgrano, this
handsomely landscaped park
covers one of the city's few
hills and was once the limit
of the Río de La Plata. Old-
timers pass the afternoon
playing chess beneath the
giant *ombú* tree, while just
downhill dog owners unleash
their pets in the gated dog run.
✉ cnr Arribeños & La
Pampa, Belgrano 🚌 15, 29,
60, 64, 118 & others ♿ fair,
some slopes

Jardín Botánico Carlos
Thays (7, D4)
Designed by French-
Argentine architect Carlos
Thays and inaugurated in
1898, this botanical garden
boasts over 3000 tree and
plant species, sculptures,
lovely iron-and-glass
greenhouses (housing cacti,
succulents, orchids, palms
and other plants) and Thay's
former mansion. Beware the
lingering scent of cat shit –
feral felines abound.

☎ 4832-6805 ✉ Av Santa
Fe 3951, Palermo $ free
🕐 8am-7pm in summer,
9am-6pm in winter 🔵 Line D,
Plaza Italia ♿ fair, dirt paths

Jardín Japonés (7, E2)
BA's beautifully maintained
Japanese gardens offer a
peaceful respite from the city
grind. Koi ponds, sculpted
shrubbery, arched red
bridges and tinkling waterfalls make for a wonderful
stroll. The restaurant (closed
Tuesday) offers delicious
sushi and tea.
☎ 4804-9141 🖥 www
.jardinjapones.com in Spanish
✉ cnr Avs Figueroa Alcorta
& Casares, Palermo $ adult
Mon-Fri US$1, Sat & Sun
US$1.35, child daily US$0.35
🕐 10am-6pm 🚌 10, 37, 67,
102, 130 ♿ excellent

Parque 3 de Febrero
(7, E2)
Also known as Bosques de
Palermo, this sprawling park
began life as the private
retreat of 19th-century
dictator Juan Manuel de
Rosas. It consists of several
beautiful park areas, with

A bird's eye view of the Palacio del Congreso

Feeding the hungry at Plaza de Mayo

ponds, pedestrian bridges and the Rosedal rose garden in and around them, making it a joy to explore. At night, Av de la Infanta Isabel transforms into BA's finest transvestite 'red light' zone.

✉ cnr Avs del Libertador & de la Infanta Isabel, Palermo 🚍 10, 34, 130 ⚕ good

Parque Centenario (3, C2)

In the western neighborhood of Caballito, Parque Centenario is a huge circular park that's great for a wander, especially on weekends when you'll find one of the city's best craft fairs (see p43). Also contains the wonderful Museo Argentino de Ciencias Naturales (p31).

✉ cnr Avs Patricias Argeninas & Coronel Díaz Vélez, Caballito 🚍 15, 34, 55, 57, 151 ⚕ excellent

Parque Lezama (5, C3)

Whether you come to kick about the giant outdoor amphitheater, drink *mate* (traditional Argentine tea) at the cement tables, visit the Museo Histórico Nacional (p22), wander the weekend craft market or just lounge beneath the shade trees, Parque Lezama is one of the

city's most interesting green spaces.

✉ cnr Defensa & Av Brasil, San Telmo 🚍 10, 22, 29, 45, 74 ⚕ good

Plaza de Mayo (4, G4)

This plaza was founded in 1580 as the city's first central plaza and was christened Plaza de Mayo after the country gained independence from Spain. It's the most symbolically important spot in the city, flanked by the Casa Rosada (p25), the Catedral Metropolitana (right) and several other important buildings. In the center stands the Pirámide de Mayo, a small obelisk commemorating the first anniversary of BA's independence from Spain.

✉ cnr Avs de Mayo & Bolívar, Microcentro 🚇 Line A, Plaza de Mayo; Line D, Catedral; Line E, Bolívar ⚕ excellent

Plaza del Congreso (4, B4)

Marking the west end of Av de Mayo, Plaza del Congreso's centerpiece is the Monumento a los Dos Congresos, which honors the congresses of 1810 in Buenos Aires and 1816 in Tucumán, both of which led to Argentine independence.

✉ cnr Avs Rivadavia & Callao, Congreso 🚇 Line A, Congreso ⚕ good

Plaza San Martín (6, D2)

Plaza San Martín is second only to Plaza de Mayo in historical importance. Blessed with grassy slopes, flanked by beautiful buildings, and shaded by giant gum, acacia, ceiba and willow trees, it wins hands down when it comes to beauty.

✉ cnr Av Santa Fe & Florida, Retiro 🚇 Line C, San Martín ⚕ fair, steps at most entrances

PLACES OF WORSHIP

Catedral Metropolitana (4, G4)

Completed in the 1820s, the austere neoclassical facade of BA's most important cathedral makes for an odd entrance into the splendid Baroque interior. The church has a

A moment of reflection – Catedral Metropolitana

JEWISH BA

Most of the estimated 250,000 Jews living in Argentina reside in Buenos Aires, making it the largest Jewish population in Latin America and one of the largest in the world. The majority live in Once, BA's version of New York's Lower East Side, where you'll find everything from Jewish-owned textile businesses to kosher pizza. After two terrorist attacks against Jewish targets, access to most Jewish sites, including the **Museo Judío Dr Salvador Kibrick** (4, D1; ☎ 4372-2474; Libertad 769) and the Templo de la Congregación Israelita have been highly restricted. Many require up to 48 hours advance notice, passport and other photo ID.

beautiful rococo main altar and contains the mausoleum of General San Martín, Argentina's greatest independence hero. Outside an eternal flame burns in his honor.
☎ 4331-2845 ⊠ cnr Av Rivadavia & San Martín, Microcentro $ free
☼ 8am-7pm Mon-Fri, 9am-7:30pm Sat & Sun ◉ Line A, Perú; Line D, Catedral; Line E, Bolívar ♿ good

Iglesia de Nuestra Señora del Pilar (2, B2)
Directly next door to the Cementerio de la Recoleta stands this lovely little baroque colonial church, a national historical monument and one of the last remaining colonial buildings in the city.
☎ 4803-6793 ⊠ Junín 1904, Recoleta $ free
☼ 8am-9pm 🚌 29, 61, 62, 92, 110 ♿ good

Iglesia Santa Catalina (4, G1)
Founded in 1745, Santa Catalina was BA's first convent, later occupied by British troops during their second invasion of the city in 1807. A peek inside reveals beautiful gilded works and a baroque altarpiece created by Spanish carver Isidro Lorea.

⊠ cnr Viamonte & San Martín, Microcentro
☼ 8am-6pm, guided tours 3pm Fri ◉ Line C, Lavalle ♿ fair, some steps

Templo de la Congregación Israelita (4, D1)
Built between 1932 and 1934, this is Argentina's largest and longest functioning synagogue. After attacks on Jewish targets in 1992 and 1994, it was outfitted with sidewalk planters (to protect against car bombs) and an iron gate. Taking photos of the synagogue is prohibited.
⊠ Libertad 769, Tribunales
☼ entrance by appt with photo ID only ◉ Line D, Tribunales ♿ difficult

MONUMENTS & PUBLIC ART

Canto al Trabajo (5, C1)
Originally in San Telmo's Plaza Dorrego, Rogelio Yrurtia's masterful bronze sculpture *Canto al Trabajo* (Song to Work) was moved in 1937 to its unfortunately inconspicuous location in Plazoleta Eva Perón.
⊠ Plazoleta Eva Perón, San Telmo 🚌 20, 33, 64, 74, 152 & others

Floralis Genérica (2, B1)
Opening its six giant metallic petals every morning and closing them again at dusk, the *Floralis Genérica* (2002) was designed and funded by architect Eduardo Catalano. Its daily springlike rebirth stands in stark contrast to the austere pillars of the Facultad de Derecho to the east.
⊠ Plaza Naciones Unidas, Recoleta 🚌 12, 124, 130

Monumento a los Españoles (7, D2)
Commanding a prime location on broad Av del Libertador, this chalk-white monument inaugurated in 1927 is one of the city's most beautiful. At its base, figures represent

Metalwork blossoms in *Floralis Genérica*

four regions of Argentina: the Pampas, the Andes, the Chaco and the Río de La Plata.
✉ cnr Avs del Libertador & Sarmiento, Palermo 🚌 10, 33, 34 Ⓜ Line D, Plaza Italia

Monumento a Sarmiento (7, D2)

Now here's an odd one. See this small statue of former Argentine president Domingo F Sarmiento, across from the giant Monumento a los Españoles? It's a Rodin.
✉ cnr Avs del Libertador & Sarmiento, Palermo 🚌 10, 33, 34 Ⓜ Line D, Plaza Italia

Monumento al General Carlos M de Alvear (2, C1)

Considered one of the city's finest monuments, this equestrian giant was created by French sculptor Emile Antoine Bourdelle. Atop sits General Alvear and below him four bronze figures represent strength, eloquence, victory and freedom.
✉ Plaza Intendente Alvear, Recoleta 🚌 17, 61, 62, 93, 110

Monumento al Libertador General San Martín (6, D2)

The Obelisco might be the capital's best-known monument, but the one

---

HOP ON THE BUS, GUS

Nothing quite compares to grinding through BA on a public bus. Hop on the No 29 in La Boca (p19) for one of the best rides of all: it barrels through La Boca and San Telmo (p18), gives you a nearly 360-degree view of the Casa Rosada (p25), cruises up Av de Mayo (p21), crosses Av 9 de Julio near the Obelisco (below) and passes the imposing Palacio de Justicia (p25) and the Palacio de las Aguas Corrientes (p25). Everything but the Obelisco will be to your left. And all for US$0.30. Get off near Plaza Italia (7, C3) for transportation back.

honoring independence hero General San Martín is its most important. When foreign dignitaries visit Buenos Aires, it's customary for them to place a wreath, usually decorated to represent the visiting country, at the base of the monument. Look for one on the north side of the statue.
✉ Plaza San Martín, Retiro Ⓜ Line C, San Martín

Obelisco (4, D2)

It's impossible to imagine BA without the Obelisco. Towering 68m above the oval Plaza de la República, it was inaugurated in 1936, on the 400th anniversary of the first Spanish settlement on the Río de la Plata. After major soccer victories, fans transform the intersection into a celebration ground.

✉ cnr Avs 9 de Julio & Corrientes, Congreso Ⓜ Line B, Carlos Pellegrini; Line D, 9 de Julio

Torre de los Ingleses (6, E1)

In 1916 BA's British community donated the 76m Torre de los Ingleses (a miniature Big Ben) to the city. During the Falklands War of 1982, the tower was the target of bombs; since then, the name of the plaza in which it stands has changed from Plaza Británica to Plaza Fuerza Aérea Argentina (Argentine Air Force Plaza).
✉ Plaza Fuerza Aérea Argentina, Retiro Ⓜ Line C, San Martín

QUIRKY BUENOS AIRES

Mercado de Pulgas (3, C1)

If you combined a Moroccan souk with a Latin American flea market, this is likely what you'd get. Wandering through the huge indoor flea market you'll find everything from fabulous '60s pop relics, clocks and lamps to jewelry, furniture and Ferris wheel seats. Everything's dusty, prices are steep, and tourists are few.

Protecting the British Crown at Torre de los Ingleses

Tierra Santa: a theme park of biblical proportions

✉ cnr Álvarez Thomas & Dorrego, Palermo $ free ⏱ 10am-6pm, until 8pm Dec-Jun 🚌 140, 151, 161, 168

Museo de Deuda Externa
Argentina recently declared the largest debt default in world history. Perhaps it's no surprise that in 2005 BA opened the first ever Museum of Foreign Debt. Exhibits change every nine months, but all are political commentaries on the havoc foreign debt has reaped on Argentina and other Latin American countries. One of a kind.
☎ 4370-6015 ✉ Centro Cultural Sabato; basement, Uriburu 763, Congreso $ free ⏱ 3-8:30pm Tue-Fri, 11am-9pm Sat Ⓜ Line D, Facultad de Medicina

Museo de la Policía Federal (4, G2)
Whoa, grab your barf bag and your sense of humor for this display of police antics, including forensic photos, dummies of murder victims, gambling and cockfighting displays and a skeleton of a police dog that died on duty.
☎ 4394-6857 ✉ 7th fl, San Martín 353, Microcentro

$ free, child under 15 not permitted ⏱ 1-6pm Tue-Fri Ⓜ Line B, Florida ♿ fair

Sonoridad Amarilla (7, A4)
A narrow winding staircase leads to several small rooms crammed with art objects, paintings, lava lamps, hookahs, Buddha heads and more. It's San Francisco's Mission District meets Alphabet City. Owners Livia and Javier offer cheap Arabic/Asian dinners as a way to introduce art to the hungry.
☎ 4777-7931
📧 sonoamarilla@fibertel .com.ar ✉ Fitz Roy 1983, Palermo Hollywood $ free ⏱ 2pm-2am Wed-Sat 🚌 21, 111, 161, 166

Tierra Santa
Forget mass. Beeline it to Tierra Santa, 'the world's first religious theme park,' whose climactic experience is a 12m Jesus that rises from the Calvary mound and opens his eyes and arms to the emotional crowd below. Fret not, there's also an Old Testament world complete with Wailing Wall, praying plastic statues and a synagogue. Amen.
☎ 4784-9551 ✉ Av Costanera R Obligado 5790

$ adults/child under 12 US$3.50/1.50 ⏱ 9am-9pm Fri, noon-11pm Sat, Sun & holidays Apr-Nov, 4pm-12.30am Fri-Sun Dec-Mar 🚌 28, 33, 37, 42, 45, 160 ♿ good

BUENOS AIRES FOR CHILDREN

BA is a wonderful city to visit with children. It is safe, and porteños are always friendly toward youngsters. You can find family-style restaurants everywhere, and dragging the littlies in is completely acceptable. As with most places, however, more upmarket restaurants are generally averse to children, especially in the evening.

There are heaps of kids' activities on offer in the capital, from museums to theater. Pick up a copy of *Planetario*, available for free at most tourist kiosks. It's loaded with activities and ads for child-related services. Buenos Aires' cultural centers (p24) often stage children's shows and offer interesting classes and workshops. For a fun pit stop, take the kids and challenge them to a game of checkers while you drink a beer and listen to house music at Acabar (p60), where you all can party.

Child-friendly places throughout this book are identified with the icon 🅰.

Jardín Zoológico (7, D3)
Built on the site of provincial governor Juan Manuel de Rosas' former *estancia* (traditional grazing estate), the city zoo makes for an excellent wander with the kiddos. Some of the enclosures are a bit tough to take, but zoological research *is* conducted here. Unless you have the kids in tow, forget the special exhibit tickets – the US$2 admission is enough.
☎ 4011-9900/9999 ☐ zoo servicios@cieargentina.com.ar ✉ cnr Avs Las Heras & Sarmiento ⑤ US$2-3.50, children under 12 free ⏱ 10am-5pm Tue-Sun, until 6pm in summer ⊙ Line D, Plaza Italia ⑤ excellent 🚼

Museo Argentino de Ciencias Naturales (3, C2)
West of the center in the huge Parque Centenario, you'll find this excellent natural science museum where you can turn the kiddos loose on displays of meteorites, rocks and minerals, seashells, insects, shark models and dinosaur replicas.
☎ 4982-1154/4494 ✉ Ángel Gallardo 470, Caballito ⑤ US$0.75 ⏱ 2-7pm 🚌 15, 36, 55, 105 ⑤ good 🚼

Museo Argentino del Títere (5, A1)
This puppet museum has a small collection of (surprise) puppets from Africa, Europe and Asia, some of which date to 1936. But the real treat is the theater. Take the kids here weekends at 4pm and enjoy the show.
☎ 4304-4376 ☐ www .museoargdeltitere.com.ar

in Spanish ✉ Piedras 905 ⑤ free ⏱ 3-6pm Tue-Sun ⊙ Line C, Independencia ⑤ good, one step 🚼

Museo de los Niños (3, D2)
Take the little ones down to this children's museum inside Shopping Abasto (p39) and turn them loose on the miniature city inside. It's complete with post office, hospital, TV station, supermarket and even a port.
☎ 4861-2325 ☐ www .museoabasto.org.ar in Spanish ✉ Mercado Abasto, Av Corrientes 3247 ⑤ 2 adults with 1/2 children US$5/7 ⏱ 1-8pm Tue-Sun ⊙ Line B, Carlos Gardel ⑤ fair 🚼

Museo Participativo de Ciencias (2, B1)
Another great one for the kids, this participatory science museum (where *not* touching is forbidden) houses interactive displays that focus on fun and learning. Inside the Centro Cultural Recoleta.
☎ 4807-3456 ☐ www.mpc .org.ar in Spanish ✉ Junín 1930, Recoleta ⑤ US$2 ⏱ 3:30-7:30pm in summer, 12:30-7:30pm Mon-Fri, 3:30-7:30pm Sat & Sun in winter 🚌 29, 61, 62, 92, 110 🚼

Parque de la Costa
You can never go wrong with an amusement park, and

Tigre's Parque de la Costa is no exception. No matter what your age, you're bound to find fun here. You padres and madres will dig the hanging-car roller coaster and the pendulum free fall. See p36 for information on Tigre.
☎ 4002-6000 ☐ www .parquedelacosta.com.ar in Spanish ✉ Vivanco 1509, Tigre ⑤ incl rides US$7, concession US$6 ⏱ 11am-7pm Fri-Sun, daily in Jan 🚆 Tren de la Costa from Estación Maipú or Mitre line from Retiro ⑤ good 🚼

Parque Temaikén
Buenos Aires' premier zoo lies outside the city limits and makes for a delightfully laid-back afternoon stroll. Over 200 species, including tigers, pumas, various reptiles and a pygmy hippo, all roam the natural and handsomely landscaped enclosures making for a fairly guilt-free experience. Stroller rentals are available.
☎ (03488) 436-900 ☐ www.temaiken.com.ar in Spanish ✉ Ruta Provincial 25, Escobar ⑤ adult/child under 10 US$5/3.50 ⏱ 10am-7pm in summer, 10am-6pm Tue-Sun in winter 🚌 60 'Escobar,' taxi (US$20, 30 minutes) ⑤ good 🚼

BA-BYSITTERS

Most top-end and all deluxe hotels offer babysitting services so you can break free for a bit. Otherwise contact Rosa Heber at **Babysitter Matapelet** (☎ 4823-9686, 15-5388-7669; babymetapelet@yahoo.com.ar); Rosa is a child psychologist who speaks Hebrew, French and some English. She will come to your hotel room to mind the kids while you're out.

Trips & Tours

WALKING TOURS
Walking with Borges

Argentina's greatest writer, Jorge Luis Borges (1899–1986), walked daily along pedestrianized Florida to his job as director of the Biblioteca Nacional (now the Centro Nacional de la Música). He was blind at the time. Follow his route, starting at **Borges' apartment** (**1**) at Maipú 944. Head south on Maipú and left on Paraguay. Have a coffee at **Florida Garden** (**2**), one of Borges' haunts and the intellectual cornerstone of the **Manzana Loca** (Crazy Block; **3**), named for the experimental art spaces that lined the 900 block of Florida in the 1960s.

Head south on Florida to the splendid **Galerías Pacífico** (**4**; p39), and see the art exhibits in the **Centro Cultural Borges** (**5**; p24) on the building's east side. Continuing south on Florida, stop at the café **Richmond** (**6**; p57), where Borges met with other writers and artists who together published the literary magazine *Martín Fierro*. Heading further south, glance right at Av Corrientes to see the **Obelisco** (**7**; p29). At Av de Mayo turn left to walk around **Plaza de Mayo** (**8**; p27). Head back to Florida (now Perú) and continue south past the **Manzana de las Luces** (**9**; p24). Carry on to México, and hang a left to finish at the **Centro Nacional de la Música** (**10**).

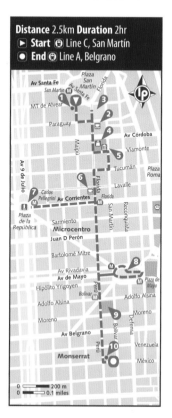

Distance 2.5km **Duration** 2hr
▶ **Start** Ⓜ Line C, San Martín
⬤ **End** Ⓜ Line A, Belgrano

Become a BA pedestrian on populous Florida

Café Crawl

Start with the basics: coffee at **El Británico** (**1**; ☎ 4300-6894; Av Brasil 899), open since 1930 and named for the British WWI vets who drank here. Head north on Defensa and right on Av San Juan to the **Museo de Arte Moderno** (**2**; p21), where you can work off some of that caffeine. Continue up Defensa and grab a bite to eat at **Bar Plaza Dorrego** (**3**; ☎ 4361-0141; Defensa 1098), whose seats have cradled the butts of Robert De Niro and Eric Clapton. Detour west on Humberto 1°, north on Bolívar and left on cobbled Estados Unidos to the lovingly restored **Café del Tiempo** (**4**; Estados Unidos 523). Head south on Perú to **El Federal** (**5**; p59), which boasts one of BA's most stunning bar tops. Walk east on Carlos Calvo to **La Coruña** (**6**; Bolívar 982), another humble classic with a comically sagging bar. After browsing the historic produce market **Mercado San Telmo** (**7**; cnr Carlos Calvo & Bolívar), swing left back onto Defensa. At Pasaje San Lorenzo check out the narrow **Casa Mínima** (**8**; Pasaje San Lorenzo) before heading north to historic **La Puerto Rico** (**9**; p59) for another well-earned coffee break.

Continue to Plaza de Mayo and west to **London City** (**10**; ☎ 4343-0328; Av de Mayo 599), where Argentine author Julio Cortázar wrote his first novel. Head further west to the city's most famous café of all, **Café Tortoni** (**11**; p59).

Distance 4km **Duration** 3-4hr
▶ **Start** 🚌 10, 22, 29, 61, 74
⏺ **End** Ⓜ Line A, Piedras

Mood lighting in Café Tortoni

Into the Gardens

After two days of doing the sidewalk slalom and dodging buses in the Microcentro, it's high time for a breather. Hello, Palermo. Start at the Beruti entrance to **Jardín Botánico Carlos Thays** (**1**; p26), and be sure to see the debauched **Saturnalia sculpture** (**2**) on the northern side of **Carlos Thays' former home** (**3**). Exit through the northwest gates, cross Av Las Heras and take a long gawk through the **Jardín Zoológico** (**4**; p31). On weekends exit the zoo on the Av del Libertador side. Otherwise, double back and take Av Sarmiento north to **Plaza Seeber** (**5**), zigzag northwest through the trees, cruise across Av del Libertador and continue northwest to the pathway along Av de la Infanta Isabel, in **Parque 3 de Febrero** (p26).

> **Distance** 5km **Duration** 4hr
> ▶ **Start** Ⓢ Line D, Scalabrini Ortiz
> ⬤ **End** 🚌 10, 37, 67, 102, 130

After passing the **paddleboat rentals** (**6**) on your right and the **Museo de Artes Plásticas Eduardo Sívori** (**7**; p21) on your left, cross the footbridge into the **Rosedal** (**8**). Sniff your way east through the rose gardens, pass by **Plaza Holanda** (**9**) and exit through the gates on Av Iraola. Cross Iraola, continue southeast across Av Sarmiento and alongside Av del Libertador. Turn north on Av Casares, and enter the peaceful **Jardín Japonés** (**10**; p26) to get your Zen on and grab a snack in the garden's **restaurant** (**11**).

Have a breather in Palermo's parks and gardens

DAY TRIPS
San Antonio de Areco (1, B3)

A serene town of crumbling colonial buildings, San Antonio de Areco is surrounded by the infinite flatness of the Pampas. Bicycles outnumber cars, traffic lights are few and men wear traditional gaucho berets and knotted scarves. You're in gaucho country, now – smack dab in the heart of it.

San Antonio sprung up in the early 1700s around a chapel built in honor of San Antonio de Padua. It's now called the **Iglesia Parroquial** (cnr Segundo Sombra & Ruiz de Arellano) and sits across from the lovely **Plaza Ruiz de Arellano**, the city's main plaza. San Antonio was the setting for Ricardo Güiraldes' famous novel *Don Segundo Sombra* (1927) which brought gaucho culture to the forefront of Argentine identity. The town's main attraction, the **Museo Gauchesco Ricardo Güiraldes** (☎ 454-780; cnr Güiraldes & Sosa; admission US$0.75; ☺ 11am-5pm Wed-Mon) is named after the author and is a sort of gaucho theme park, with an old flour mill, a mock tavern and a chapel.

Every year, during mid-November's **Día de la Tradición** (Day of Tradition), the town puts on the country's biggest gaucho celebration. It's also home to the country's best leather workers and silversmiths who craft beautiful jewelry and knives, ornate *mates* (cups for drinking *yerba mate* tea), riding crops, saddles and more. Of the numerous *talleres* (workshops), be certain to visit **Draghi** (☎ 454-207; Lavalle 387; ☺ 10:30am-1pm & 3:30-7:30pm), the workshop and store of internationally known silversmith Raúl Horacio Draghi. For chocolates and *alfajores* (classic Argentine cookies) visit **La Olla de Cobre** (☎ 453-105; Matheu 433).

INFORMATION
113km northwest of Buenos Aires
- 🚌 frequent buses (US$4, 2 hr) from Retiro bus station stop five blocks from town
- ☎ area code 02326
- ℹ tourist office (☎ 453-165; Zerboni & Arellano; ☺ 8:30am-10pm Mon-Fri, 8am-8pm Sat & Sun)
- ✕ El Almacén (Bolívar 66; ☺ closed Mon)

Sunrise, gaucho-style

MICHAEL COYNE

Tigre & the Delta (1, B3)

Once the stomping grounds for BA's upper echelons and later abandoned for the trendier beach town of Mar del Plata, Tigre remains for many por-teños the quickest way out of the beast. The town sits on the south-ern edge of the **Delta del Paraná**, a vast maze of rivers, islands and subtropical vegetation accessible by boat tours from town.

> **INFORMATION**
>
> *28km northwest of Buenos Aires*
>
> 🚃 either via regular train from Estación Retiro (Mitre line) or via Tren de la Costa (Coast Train; ☎ 4002-6000; www.trendelacosta.com.ar; US$2, 25min) from Estación Maipú (Av Maipú 2305, Olivos). For the Coast Train take the Mitre line from Retiro and transfer at Maipú.
>
> 🚌 Nos 59 or 60 to Estación Maipú (signed 'bajo,' 'alto' or 'Escobar')
>
> ℹ️ Tigre tourist office (☎ 4512-4497/4498; Mitre 35, Estación Fluvial Tigre; 🕘 9am-5pm) Pick up a local map here.
>
> 🍴 food stalls

The Tren de La Costa (Coast Train) drops you directly in front of the Parque de La Costa amuse-ment park (p31). From here you can walk five minutes to Tigre's Puerto de Frutos, a former fruit market and now a fun, family-filled portside affair with food stands, flower stalls, candy vendors and souvenir shops. The train from Estación Retiro stops in front of the **Estación Fluvial Tigre**, the main departure point for fascinating **boat tours** (US$4 to US$10) into the delta. Shuttle boats also ferry people to riverside establishments such as **Tres Bocas**, where you can wander around and check out the odd, stilted houses typical of the delta.

PARQUE NACIONAL IGUAZÚ

Simply put, Iguazú Falls are the most spectacular waterfalls on the planet. But you'll need at least three extra days to visit them from Buenos Aires to allow time to see the falls from both the Brazilian and Argentine sides – a must – and to take a boat ride into the Garganta del Diablo (Devil's Throat), the most spectacular of the hundreds of waterfalls. **Aerolíneas Argentinas** (4, F4; ☎ 0810-222-86527; www.aerolineas.com; Perú 2) and **Southern Winds** (6, D2; ☎ 4515-8600; www.sw.com.ar in Spanish; Av Santa Fe 784) both fly to the nearby town of Puerto Iguazú for US$200 round-trip. For further informa-tion, including hotels and tours, contact BA's **Secretaría de Turismo de la Nación** (6, D2; ☎ 4312-2232; www.turismo.gov.ar; Av Santa Fe 883; 🕘 9am-5pm weekdays) or the **tourist office** (☎ 03757-420800; Av Victoria Aguirre 311) in Puerto Iguazú.

MARK NEWMAN

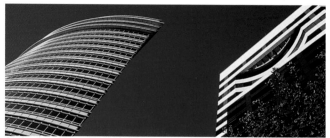
Get the edge on Buenos Aires architecture

ORGANIZED TOURS

Buenos Aires can be overwhelming. An organized tour – whether by foot, bike or bus – can provide an excellent introduction to the capital, and will help to flesh out the many nuances that make the city so fascinating. Architecture, neighborhood, soccer, history, art and cultural tours are available. The following all have English-speaking guides, but you should always arrange for one in advance, just to make sure.

Eternautas
With an enthusiastic team of historians, architects and university teachers, Eternautas is a sure bet for an outstanding tour. Three-hour to full-day tours include themes such as Evita and Peronism; the 'forgotten south' of Buenos Aires; Jewish BA; and art and architecture.
☎ 4384-7874; 15-4173-1078 🖳 www.eternautas.com 💲 2-person 3hr tour US$74 🕃 daily

La Bicicleta Naranja (5, C1)
Rent bikes and peddle the streets yourself or choose from one of four guided bike tours: San Telmo/La Boca, the riverfront, northern Buenos Aires, and Reserva Ecológica Costanera Sur.
☎ 4362-1104 🖳 www.labicicletanaranja.com.ar in Spanish ✉ Pasaje Giuffra 308, San Telmo 💲 bike rental per hour/day US$2/10, per subsequent days US$5; 1-2hr guided bike tours US$10, 3-4 hrs US$19 🕃 tours at 9:30am & 2:30pm

Cicerones
Through its online registration form, Cicerones matches your interests and language needs with one of its team of volunteer guides. Fill out the form online, and Cicerones will match you with someone within two days. If you're only in town for a couple days, set things up before you leave home. It's an outstanding operation.
☎ 4330-0800, 4431-9892 🖳 www.cicerones.org.ar 💲 free 🕃 daily

Tangol (6, E3)
Long in the business, Tangol offers conventional city tours (one combines a boat ride on the Río de la Plata), as well as a 'BA by Night' tour, *estancia* (traditional grazing estate) trips and excursions to Tigre. It also offers guided packages to soccer games in the city.
☎ 4312-7276 🖳 www.tangol.com ✉ Florida 971, local 59, Retiro 💲 US$9-35 🕃 daily

Urban Biking
Four interesting young Argentines run this pedaling outfit, taking folks everywhere from Tigre to La Plata (the provincial capital) and around the city at night. English is spoken, and tours include helmet, locks and child seats if necessary. Reservations are a must.
☎ 4855-5103 🖳 www.urbanbiking.com in Spanish 💲 US$20-50 🕃 daily

Wow Argentina (6, D2)
Husband-and-wife team Matías and Cintia offer personalized three- to four-hour tours that take in BA's most important sights with a dash of history, culture and the daily life of BA. You can tailor your tour to suit your interests as well.
☎ 15-5603-2926 🖳 www.wowargentina.com.ar ✉ Santa Fe 882, 2F 💲 1-2 people US$95 🕃 daily

Shopping

Buenos Aires offers the perfect opportunity to whip out the old in Rome…' excuse to justify a serious spending spree. Porteños (B dents) *love* to shop. The peso's drop in purchasing power seems affected nothing. They're out in hordes with handbags from Re Palermo every day but Sunday (when it's *almost* as fun to window and there's no reason not to join them. With the current exchange r

all that Buenos Aires has to offer, shopping could easily consume your entire trip. When it comes to fashion, the sheer number of local designers and single-brand boutiques is mind-boggling. The country is famous for its leather, with some of the best quality in the world. Just take a stroll down Florida (and get ready to fend off the flyers).

Argentina is also known for its silverwork. Jewelry, especially bracelets and pendants with traditional motifs, make excellent buys. Knives, with handles of ornately carved silver or intricately woven leather, are a part of Argentina's gaucho past (and its obsession with meat) and are sold everywhere. *Mate* (traditional Argentine tea) drinking vessels make great souvenirs and range from cheap, traditional hollowed-out *calabazas* (gourds) to ornate silver goblets. Look out for red-and-black wool ponchos (shawls for men) from the northwest of Argentina. Argentina is also obsessed with horses, so you'll find plenty of high-quality horse gear.

Get all of your shopping out of the way before Sunday, when nearly everything but the shopping centers closes, and forget any midnight buys the night before your flight

SHOPPING AREAS

For the city's hippest, hottest fa hit **Palermo Viejo**. **Av Santa** pecially the stretch east of Libert fers over 30 blocks of clothes-sh madness. For upscale boutiques duce yourself to **Av Alvear** in Re The block of **Av Murillo** in th (in Villa Crespo) is the land of l outlets (bargain *hard*). For a 'Latin American' (ie chaotic) ence, head to **Once**, especially th around the intersection of Avs redon and Rivadavia. Local de: continue to open boutique co **San Telmo**, making it a great to score cheap, fashionable clot along with the usual antiques.

Gloriously restored Shopping Abas

home. Monday through Saturday, shops generally open from 10am to around 8pm. Shopping centers stay open until 10pm. cards are widely accepted; see p88 for reasons why you might pref At most places, sales tax is already figured into the price. Some sho tax refund vouchers that you can cash in at the airport when yo the country. Only the most tourist-oriented stores will ship, thou shipping costs can nullify any deal you might have gotten.

SHOPPING CENTERS

Galería Bond Street (2, C3)
The soft buzz of tattoo guns hum from the dozen tattoo parlors while BA punkers shop to funky beats pouring out of the rock shops, hipster stores, raver shops, and more. Clothes, paraphernalia and graffiti-covered walls make for some great urban shopping.
✉ Av Santa Fe 1670, Recoleta ⏰ 10am-9pm Mon-Sat ⓜ Line D, Callao

Galerías Pacífico (4, F1)
Built in 1889 by Paris department store Bon Marché, this exquisite shopping center sat empty for years before being restored in 1992 to its present state. More impressive than the top-name stores inside are the vaulted ceilings, painted by five renowned Argentine artists, including Antonio Berni.
☎ 5555-5110 💻 www.galeriaspacifico.com.ar in Spanish ✉ cnr Florida & Av Córdoba ⏰ 10am-9pm Mon-Sat, noon-9pm Sun ⓜ Line C, San Martín

Patio Bullrich
Small but swanky Patio Bullrich is the place where cash-laden porteños come to drop their dough and drink coffees at one of several chichi onsite cafés. A number of BA's top designers have shops here.
☎ 4814-7400/7500 💻 www.shoppingbullrich.com.ar ✉ Av Libertador 750, Recoleta ⏰ 10am-9pm 🚌 17, 61, 62, 92, 124, 130

SIZING THINGS UP
Clothing sizes in Buenos Aires are all over the map, especially for women's brands. A women's size 3 at one store might be a medium at another store and a size 'too big to stock' at another. In fact, women who are a hair wider than a rail may find their sizes hard to come by, period. Paying no heed to simple economics (not to mention a recently passed law requiring stores to stock larger sizes), many stores only stock clothing big enough to fit a stick. Remember, you're not alone in your search for something bigger. Men's clothes are generally in European sizes, but sometimes in US sizes. Shoes for everyone follow European sizes.

Shopping Abasto (3, D2)
Worth a visit if only to see the restored landmark building that once housed the city's main produce market. It now houses over 200 modern clothing stores, a food court and a children's museum (p31). Outside, a statue honors tango composer Carlos Gardel who once lived in the neighborhood.
☎ 4959-3400 💻 www.abasto-shopping.com.ar in Spanish ✉ cnr Av Corrientes & Anchorena, Abasto ⏰ 10am-10pm ⓜ Line B, Carlos Gardel

CLOTHING & ACCESSORIES

Women's Fashions
Calma Chicha (7, B5)
Like many top Palermo designers, Calma Chicha takes its inspiration from Argentine traditions, crafting stylish clothing and throwing kitschy Argentine bric-a-brac in for fun. Check out the colorfully embroidered *bombachas* (Argentine gaucho pants) and camouflage pajamas. The branch around the corner (7, B5; Honduras 4925) deals in housewares.
☎ 4831-1818 💻 www.calmachicha.com in Spanish ✉ Gurruchaga 1580, Palermo Viejo ⏰ 10am-8pm Mon-Sat, 2-8pm Sun 🚌 15, 55, 57, 140, 151, 168

Cat Ballou (2, C2)
Esteemed designers Alicia Goñi and Florencia Pieres kick out some of the city's most fashionable clothing and jewelry, allowing BA's hip upper echelons to gypsy things up. Pieres' splendid, fairly priced jewelry combines fabric and jewels with an exquisitely beautiful, ragtag result.
☎ 4811-9792 ✉ Av Alvear 1702, Recoleta ⏰ 11am-8pm Mon-Fri, 10:30am-4:30pm Sat 🚌 17, 59, 67, 75, 102

Gabriella Capucci (6, C1)
After living in Los Angeles for 10 years, designer Geraldine Komcar returned to BA to take over her mother's store, filling it with her wildly funky shirts, skirts, handbags and jewelry that combine LA

Purring with style, Cat Ballou

glitz, kitsch and Argentine icons. Great gifts for the girlfriends back home.
☎ 4815-3636 ✉ Av Alvear 1477, Retiro ◷ 10:30am-8pm Mon-Sat, closed 2-3pm Sat 🚍 17, 59, 67, 75, 102

Humawaca (7, C5)
Award-winning BA designer Ingrid Gutman brings functionality and eye-popping modernist design to Argentine leather (both hairy and hairless), producing purses, backpacks and wallets that are beautifully unique. Most have clever interchangeable features (such as reversible leather-versus-waterproof bags) that allow you to modify your sack to suit your situation.
☎ 4832-2662 🖥 www .humawaca.com ✉ El Salvador 4692, Palermo Viejo ◷ 11am-8pm Mon-Sat 🚍 34, 55, 166

Juana de Arco (7, B5)
Since 1998, designer Mariana Cortés has been dazzling her Palermo visitors with colorful, sexy, often whacky and always fun women's underwear, clothing and shoes. It's truly a delight to browse the clothing (be sure to go down stairs), which is often inspired by traditional Argentine country garb.
☎ 4833-1621 🖥 www .juanadearco.net ✉ El Salvador 4762, Palermo Viejo ◷ 10:30am-8pm Mon-Sat 🚍 34, 55, 166

Maria Vazquez
Maroons, seaweed-greens and earth tones dominate the color schemes of Maria Vazquez's ultrafashionable yet surprisingly affordable women's party wear. Pick up a fake fur coat to wear over a crinoline layered dress and step out in style. Hey, if it's good enough for Shakira…
☎ 4815-6333 🖥 www .mvzmariavazquez.com.ar in Spanish ✉ Libertad 1632, Recoleta ◷ 10am-8pm Mon-Fri, to 6pm Sat 🚍 17, 59, 67, 75, 102

Moebius (5, C2)
Fifteen local designers sew up funky, retro-inspired clothing for women and men at this highly affordable San Telmo boutique. The 1950s-style, patched-together skirts bring down the house. Sweaters, funky T-shirts and kitschy 'pleather' shoulder bags and wallets all make great gifts.
☎ 4361-2893 ✉ Defensa 1356, San Telmo 🖥 moebiusropa@yahoo .com.ar ◷ 3-8pm Wed-Sat, 11am-8:30pm Sun 🚍 10, 22, 24, 29, 39, 45, 74

Nadine Zlotogora (7, C5)
The beautifully unique – and often unisex – clothing of Nadine Zlotogora ranges from flared pants (think Northern Soul with a sailor's touch) and far-out jackets, to printed dress shirts with crinoline outer lining and custom Converse. You're bound to feel footloose in this stuff. Go, gypsy, go!
☎ 4831-4203 ✉ El Salvador 4638, Palermo Viejo ◷ 11am-8pm Mon-Sat 🚍 15, 57, 110, 141, 160

Rapsodia (7, B5)
Girls, leave your party clothes at home and stock up here, where bohemian chic is fun, functional and flirtatious. Cocktail dresses,

Bohemian Rapsodia

LUST FOR LINGERIE

Styling yourself out with matching lingerie for every night of the week might break the bank back home, but in BA, a pair of hot Palermo panties will set you back only US$5 to US$8. Sizes tend to run painfully small, but give 'em a go. Try **Juana de Arco** (opposite), **Amor Latino** (7, B5; ☎ 4831-6787; www.amor-latino.com.ar in Spanish; Gorriti 4925; 🕐 11am-8pm Mon-Sat) and **Bendita Tú Eres** (7, B5; ☎ 4834-6123; Thames 1555; 🕐 noon-8pm Mon-Sat). **Glam** (7, B5; ☎ 4831-5613; Armenia 1460; 🕐 11am-8pm Mon-Sat) stocks sexy sequined undergarments, sporty underwear and eye-popping disco skirts too. Mua!

flowing shirts, sweaters, satiny scarves and Rapsodia's must-have jeans (the ones with the wings embroidered on the butts) are all available at great prices.
☎ 4832-5363 🖥 www.rapsodia.com.ar ✉ El Salvador 4757, Palermo Viejo 🕐 10am-9pm Mon-Sat, noon-9pm Sun 🚌 15, 57, 110, 141, 160

Tramando (2, C2)
Designer Martín Churba creates some seriously unique clothing with a sex-you-up style entirely his own. You'll stand out in *any* crowd donning these duds. The recent spring lineup ranged from sliced up skirts, shiny tank-top body suits for men, skintight dresses and mesh skirts. Everything is made on the premises.
☎ 4811-0465 🖥 www.tramando.com ✉ Rodríguez Peña 1973, Recoleta 🕐 10:30am-8:30pm Mon-Sat 🚌 17, 59, 67, 75, 102

Uma (7, B5)
Women, hold off on spending your wad until you check out Uma, where leather jackets,

shoes and handbags are all knockout good looking, versatile and wonderfully wearable to boot. There are also branches in Patio Bullrich and Galerías Pacífico.
☎ 4832-2122 ✉ Honduras 5225, Palermo Viejo 🕐 11am-8pm Mon-Sat 🚌 34, 55, 166

Menswear

Buenos Aires' menswear lines tend to lean toward the understated. Fellas who require some more panache in their pants should check out Nadine Zlotogora and Tramando.

El Cid (7, B5)
A straightforward line of pants, dress shirts, leather jackets, leather bags and shoes is on offer here for the dude who wants smart without compromising style. Lots of pinstriped dress shirts and plenty of hip sports coats. There's a branch in San Telmo (5, C1; ☎ 4300-6682; Defensa 941).
☎ 4832-3339 ✉ Gurruchaga 1732,

Palermo Viejo 🕐 10am-8pm Mon-Sat, noon-6pm Sun 🚌 34, 36, 55, 161

Etiqueta Negra (2, C2)
C'mon, the designer has a 1960 convertible Jaguar XKE 150 parked in the store – he *knows* what's up. Gentlemen, take your pick from sweatshirts, suits, chinos, dress shirts, leather jackets and more, all sewn up in muted colors with an eye for simplicity. One of BA's hottest.
☎ 4814-7430 ✉ Posadas 1229, Recoleta 🕐 10am-9pm 🚌 17, 59, 67, 75, 102

Felix (7, B5)
Caught somewhere between skatewear and preppy attire, Felix offers trendy, casual dress shirts, T-shirts, pants and scarves for a put-together, kick-around-town look. Prices are good.
☎ 4832-1670 ✉ Gurruchaga 1670, Palermo Viejo 🕐 11am-8pm Mon-Sat, 2-7pm Sun 🚌 15, 55, 57, 140, 151, 168

Hermanos Estebecorena (7, A3)
For stylish, inconspicuous, comfortable and totally functional men's streetwear and dress clothes, head straight to Hermanos Estebecorena, where the threads – from reversible bomber jackets and raincoats to shoes and pants – are a pleasure to wear.
☎ 4772-2145 🖥 www.hermanosestebecorena.com in Spanish ✉ El Salvador 5960, Palermo Hollywood 🕐 11am-9pm Mon-Sat 🚌 15, 57, 110, 141, 160

LEATHER & SHOES

28 Sport (7, A4)

Forget Fluvog. Get yourself over to 28 Sport and lace up a pair of these handmade beauties, designed after an old Argentine boot brand with a punky street-stompin' edge. You simply don't find quality like this these days. There's a one-offs shelf to boot. Prices range from US$65 to US$115.
☎ 4776-6007
🖳 www.28sport.com
✉ Fitz Roy 1962, Palermo

Hollywood ☺ 11am-1:30pm & 2:30pm-8pm Mon-Sat
🚌 15, 21, 29, 36, 59, 60, 64, 152 & others

de Maria

Pointy flats, heels and knee-high boots are all handmade and crafted with bright colors, while the designs hint at footwear for wealthy gypsies. Handbags and jackets take backseat to the shoes, but, boy, they are slick too.
☎ 4815-5001 ✉ Libertad 1655, Recoleta ☺ 10am-9pm Mon-Fri, 10am-6pm Sat
🚌 17, 59, 67, 75, 102

GOTTA GET IT!

You bought the leather jacket and traditional silver jewelry. So now what? Perfectly porteño gifts to bring home include the following.

Diego Maradona wine – available in bottle or box in most supermarkets.

Dulce de leche – Argentina's famed milk caramel; Chimbote is considered the best, but standard brand Sancor is creamier.

Mafalda – Argentina's favorite comic girl; available in English at most bookshops.

Mate & bombilla – the ubiquitous gourd and straw for drinking *mate* 'traditional Argentine tea.'

Pinguino – traditional ceramic wine pitcher in the shape of a penguin; available at La Dorita (p54)

Rapsodia jeans – so what if they're *so* five-minutes-ago, their winged back pockets will style you back home.

Tango shoes – who cares if you can't dance!

Bring home the national beverage

Prüne (6, E3)

Here's where you go for a handbag, ladies. Styles are chic and quality is superb. If you can make it past the purses you'll find fabulous leather jackets starting at around US$175, a steal considering the work.
☎ 4893-2641 ✉ Florida 963, Retiro ☺ 10am-8pm Mon-Sat, 11am-6pm Sun
🚇 Line C, San Martín

Tango Brujo (4, E1)

Tangophiles who want to put a cutting edge on their step should visit Tango Brujo, which makes modern versions of tango shoes (Velcro tennies with heels!) along with beautiful traditional styles. Lots of great clothes and accessories too.
☎ 4325-8264 🖳 www.tangobrujo.com.ar in Spanish ✉ Esmeralda 754, Microcentro ☺ 10am-9pm Mon-Sat 🚇 Line C, Lavalle

Welcome Marroquinería (6, E3)

Long in the business, Welcome stocks a conservative line of men's and women's leatherwear, shoes and bags, all of it high quality and built for everyday use.
☎ 4312-8911 🖳 www.welcome-leather.com.ar
✉ MT de Alvear 500, Retiro ☺ 10am-2pm & 3-7:30pm Mon-Fri, 10am-1:30pm Sat
🚌 17, 59, 67, 75, 102

DESIGN & HOME ACCESSORIES

30 Quarenta (6, D1)

Art nouveaux meets Argentine modern at this funky design shop, with plenty of

coffee-table-type accessories (playing cards, coasters, paper weights etc) scattered among the bigger stuff.
☎ 4326-1065 ✉ Arroyo 890, Retiro 🕑 11am-7:30pm Mon-Fri 🚇 Line C, San Martín

Buenos Aires Design
(2, B1)
Although you'll likely refrain from dragging home a designer kitchen sink, this top-end interior design mall, featuring everything from ultrachic furniture, art and appliances to Asian rugs, designer clothes and African wall-hangings, is truly worth a browse. It's the main outlet for many of BA's top designers.
☎ 5777-6000 ✉ Av Pueyrredón 2501, Recoleta 🕑 10am-9pm Mon-Sat, noon-9pm Sun 🚌 17, 61, 62, 67, 92, 110

Materia Urbana (5, C1)
Once you're overwhelmed by San Telmo antiques, beeline it to this superb design boutique (a rarity in these parts), which sells beautiful pieces by over 130 Argentine artists. Jewelry, clothes and art objects are all in packable sizes. Don't miss the deer-hide handbags with polished antler handles.
☎ 4361-5265 🖥 www .materiaurbana.com in

GRANDMA'S ATTIC
San Telmo is ground zero for antiques in Buenos Aires, and Defensa has almost door-to-door antique shops. Most goodies are far too big to fit into a suitcase (unless you can creatively squeeze in a 1938 Norton or a merry-go-round horse), but for fun browsing check out the following:

Gabriel del Campo (5, C1; ☎ 4361-2061; gabrieldelcampo@hotmail.com; Defensa 990; 🕑 10am-7pm)

Imhotep (5, C1; ☎ 4862-9298; Defensa 916; 🕑 11am-6pm Sun-Fri)

Gil Antiguedades (5, C2; ☎ 4361-5019; Humberto 1° 412; 🕑 11am-1pm & 3-7pm)

Spanish ✉ Defensa 707, San Telmo 🕑 11am-7pm Tue-Sun 🚌 10, 22, 29, 45, 86 & others

MARKETS

Feria Artesanal Plaza Intendente Alvear (2, C1)
Just outside Cementerio de la Recoleta (p16), this huge, meandering crafts fair is the city's biggest. Popcorn vendors vie with craft stalls and buskers for a mind-boggling array of art, photographs, tango knickknacks, jewelry, scarves and more. It makes for a perfect postnecropolis weekend afternoon.
✉ Plaza Intendente Alvear, Recoleta 🕑 10am-8pm Sat & Sun 🚌 17, 29, 61, 62, 67, 92, 93, 110

Feria de Arte Palermo Viejo (7, B5)
Flanked by cafés with outdoor tables, Palermo Viejo's Plaza Serrano transforms into an outdoor art fair featuring the works of local painters. It's a great chance to pick up a piece of reasonably priced art and talk to the painters themselves.
✉ Plaza Serrano, Palermo Viejo 🕑 11am-7pm Sat & Sun

Feria de Parque Centenario (3, C2)
Rivaling the feria at Plaza Intendente Alvear in terms of size, this one definitely wins out in terms of variety: everything from antiques to women's nylons can be found, along with a stretch of used bookstalls and plenty of arts and crafts.
✉ Parque Centenario, Caballito 🕑 9am-6pm Sat & Sun 🚌 15, 34, 55, 57, 151

Feria de Parque Rivadavia (3, C3)
Used bookstalls and record dealers compete with heavy-metal bootleggers and

Plan your dream home at Buenos Aires Design

pirated CD booths for some great multimedia browsing. Everything from tango to Iron Maiden videos can be found. ✉ Parque Rivadavia, cnr Avs Rivadavia & Acoyte, Caballito ⏱ 9am-6:30pm ⦿ Line A, Acoyte

ARTS & CRAFTS

Guido (6, B1)
The odd opening hours alone should give you an idea of the character of this silver and crafts shop, run by a kind old man who stocks every imaginable gaucho implement you can think of: knives, *mate* paraphernalia, belt buckles, kettles, books, leather boxes, dice shakers… One of a kind. ☎ 4812-3939 ✉ Monte-video 1613, Recoleta ⏱ 2:50-8:08pm Mon-Fri 🚌 17, 59, 67, 75, 102

Kelly's
Stocking everything from cowhides and Mapucho ponchos to *mate* paraphernalia, silverwork, knives and indigenous crafts, this is the place to go for beautiful, high-end Argentine souvenirs. ☎ 4311-9339 ✉ Juana Manso 1596 ⏱ 10am-8pm Tue-Sat, noon-8pm Sun 🚌 2

Tierra Adentro (6, C1)
Working with nonprofit organizations to help preserve indigenous communities

throughout South America, Tierra Adentro sells beauti-fully handcrafted blankets, statues, wall hangings and other aboriginal crafts. ☎ 4393-8552 🖳 www .tierraadentro.info ✉ Arroyo 946 ⏱ 10am-8pm Mon-Fri, 10am-6pm Sat 🚌 17, 59, 62, 75, 93, 152

MUSIC & BOOKS

Club de Tango (4, C3)
Home to a truly amazing array of tango memorabilia, includ-ing posters, cards, videos, books and CDs. The posters and postcards (beautiful reprints of old tango sheet-music covers) are some of the coolest art souvenirs you'll find anywhere. Prices are excellent. Take the elevator to the 5th floor and find office 114. ☎ 4372-7251 🖳 www .clubdetango.com.ar in Spanish ✉ Paraná 123, Microcentro ⏱ 11am-6pm Mon-Fri ⦿ Line A, Sáenz Peña

El Ateneo (2, B3)
Even if you don't need a book, pop into Ateneo's flagship store, the biggest bookstore in South America and a treat for the eyes. It occupies the restored Grand Splendid theater, built in 1919 and now complete with bookshelves in the balconies, reading nooks in the boxes and a café on stage.

☎ 4813-6052 ✉ Av Santa Fe 1860, Recoleta ⏱ 9am-10pm ⦿ Line D, Callao

Gandhi Galerna (4, B2)
Among the philosophy, history and art books at this thinker-gatherer bookstore, you'll find a large selection of tango reads (mostly in Spanish) and an excellent range of Latin American music CDs, from *rock nacional* (Argentine rock) to Brazilian beats. ☎ 4374-7574 🖳 www .galernalibros.com in Spanish ✉ Av Corrientes 1743, Microcentro ⏱ 10am-10pm Mon-Thu, 10am-midnight Fri & Sat, 4-10pm Sun ⦿ Line B, Callao

Tienda Cultural (4, G4)
For books on BA, it's hard to beat this outlet for books published by the Buenos Aires Ministry of Culture. Most are in Spanish, but choices include picture-filled guides to BA architecture, public art, historic cafés, street names and more. ☎ 4329-9669 ✉ Av de Mayo 575, Microcentro ⏱ 11am-8pm Mon-Fri, noon-8pm Sat ⦿ Line A, Perú; Line D, Catedral

Zival's (4, B3)
Only the BA music chain Musimundo rivals this inde-pendent music store in terms of size, but with listening stations, books, sheet music and an unbelievable variety of tango CDs, Zival's blows doors on its competitor. It's one of the best music stores in town. ☎ 4371-7500 🖳 www .zivals.com ✉ Av Callao 395, Microcentro ⏱ 9:30am-10pm Mon-Sat ⦿ Line B, Callao

Tread the boards at El Ateneo bookstore

FOOD & DRINK

El Fenix (6, C2)
This store stocks everything from traditional Argentine *dulce de batata* (candied sweet potato) and jams, to fine wines and gourmet *dulce de leche* (Argentina's famed milk caramel). Take home a triple-pack of Luigi Bosca wine and a can of El Chimbote *dulce de leche* and your friends will love you forever.
☎ 4811-0363 ✉ Av Santa Fe 1199, Retiro 🕙 8am-8pm Mon-Fri, 8am-2pm Sat
🚌 10, 21, 39, 67, 152 & others

Ligier (6, D2)
There's an outrageous variety of Argentine wines here, with a sizable selection of *malbecs* (Argentina's signature red), mostly in the US$10 to US$25 range.
☎ 4515-0126 🖥 www .ligier.com.ar in Spanish ✉ Av Santa Fe 800, Retiro 🕙 9:30am-8:30pm Mon-Sat, closed 2-4pm Sat
🚇 Line C, San Martín

Winery (4, G2)
Spacious and modern, Winery stocks an excellent selection of Argentine varietals and boasts a wine bar so you can taste before you buy (you pay by the glass). Branches around the city include one at Retiro (6, E3; cnr Tres Sargentos & Av LN Alem).
☎ 4394-2200 🖥 www .winery.com.ar in Spanish ✉ Av Corrientes 302, Microcentro 🕙 9am-9pm Mon-Fri, 9am-2pm Sat
🚇 Line B, LN Alem

FOR CHILDREN

Grisino (7, C5)
Even littlies will enjoy shopping here. The huge selection of colorful and funky kids clothing (from ages two to 10) includes corduroy jumpsuits and whacky T-shirts.
✉ Malabia 1784, Palmero Viejo 🕙 11am-8:30pm Mon-Sat, 1-8:30pm Sun
🚌 15, 57, 110, 141, 160

Owoko (7, C5)
Named after the cartoon planet plucked from the clothing creator's head, Owoko sells kids' T-shirts, pants and pajamas all decorated with bug-eyed cartoon characters donning catchy attire to match the season. For ages newborn to nine.
🖥 www.owoko.com.ar in Spanish ✉ El Salvador 4694, Palermo Viejo 🕙 11am-8pm Mon-Sat 🚌 15, 57, 110, 141, 160

SPECIALIST STORES

Aynié (7, B1)
For polo gear (Argentina is famous for the stuff) you can either buy the overpriced goods along Florida or you can shop here, next to the polo grounds. Along with loads of specialty riding gear, you'll find jewelry, shoes, clothes and leather work as well.
☎ 4771-0050 ✉ Ortega y Gasset 1539 🕙 9am-8pm Mon-Fri, 10am-1pm Sat
🚌 64

El Remanso (6, D3)
Polo hats and saddles, riding crops, leather riding boots, silverwork, gloves, vests – you name it, this is the place for traditional upper-end riding and polo gear.
☎ 4312-1879 ✉ Esmeralda 1018, Retiro 🕙 9am-7pm Mon-Fri, 10am-5pm Sat
🚇 Line C, San Martín

Papelera Palermo (7, B5)
Stocking artsy postcards and journals, this place also offers classes in paper-making and other things for kids, and origami and other classes for adults.
☎ 4833-3081/3672 🖥 www.papelerapalermo .com.ar in Spanish ✉ Honduras 4945 🕙 1-8pm Mon-Sat, 2-8pm Sun 🚌 15, 55, 57, 140, 151, 168

BUENOS AIRES READS
Jorge Luis Borges' *Fervor de Buenos Aires* (partially published in English in *Selected Poems*), is one of Borges' only books set in BA, rather than in the writer's imaginary worlds. *Hopscotch,* by BA's other literary great, Julio Cortázar, jumps between BA and Paris. Journalist Miranda France's *Bad Times in Buenos Aires* humorously (though sometimes overbearingly) recounts her bad times in BA in the 1980s. For the straight dope on Diego Maradona, read Jimmy Burns' excellent *Hand of God.* For a glimpse into the life of Argentina's beloved Evita, check out Julie M Taylor's *Eva Perón: The Myths of a Woman.*

Eating

There's never been a better time to eat in Buenos Aires. Only a decade ago, beef, pasta and pizza – mainstays of the porteño (BA resident) diet – seemed the only things available. Now, a savvy new generation of restaurateurs and chefs, looking inside as much as outside the country for gastronomic inspiration, are opening fabulous new eateries on a regular basis. The result has been the exciting development of Argentine nouvelle cuisine, which puts modern spins on everything from *cordero patagónico* (Patagonian lamb), *jabalí* (wild boar) and *ciervo* (venison) to pizza and fish.

Of course, there are still countless old *bodegones,* the old-time eateries so classic of Buenos Aires, as well as pizza houses, pasta joints and – best of all – *parrillas* (grill restaurants). No trip to Buenos Aires is complete without experiencing a *parrilla,* where Argentina's world-famous beef is heaped onto your plate fresh from the grill (see p12).

Argentina also produces world-class wines, and restaurants are often the best places to sample them. An outstanding bottle of Argentine *malbec* (the country's signature red) can cost less than US$10. You can knock that price above US$50 if you really want to splash out.

Argentines eat late. Restaurants rarely open for dinner before 8pm,

LA CUENTA (THE BILL)

With the peso hovering around three to the US dollar, eating out in Buenos Aires is cheap. Two people can sit down at an outstanding restaurant, order one or two appetizers, two main courses, a dessert and four cocktails and walk away, tip included, only US$50 in the hole. At cheaper places you can lunch well for under US$5 per person. The pricing symbols used in this chapter indicate the cost of a two-course meal for one person, excluding drinks.

$	under $5
$$	$5-10
$$$	$10-15
$$$$	over $15

and tables generally don't fill until after 10pm. Reservations at swankier restaurants are advised, but many places don't take them after 9:30pm, and you'll often have to wait if you show up after 10pm.

Nearly all hotels serve breakfast, but if you do venture out for your morning meal, you'll find it in cafés. It won't be a big egg meal; porteños almost invariably eat a light breakfast of *medialunas* (croissants) or *facturas* (pastries) with coffee.

Tipping 10% is customary and highly appreciated, even when a *cubierto* (silverware charge of US$0.60 to US$2 per person) is already tacked on, which is often the case in upscale restaurants. Most restaurants have a nonsmoking section, but that simply means one side of you will be smoke-free; request *sector no-fumador.* Restaurants in this book with real (not just token) nonsmoking sections get the ☒ icon.

MICROCENTRO & RETIRO

Azzurra (4, G2)
Modern Argentine $$$$
Although the nouvelle Argentine fare (rib-eye steaks, rack of lamb, pastas and more) pales in comparison to the 19th-floor view over Puerto Madero and the Río de la Plata, the soft romantic atmosphere makes dining here a true delight. It's sophisticated yet casual enough for jeans and well worth the price tag.
☎ 4893-2141
✉ Av Corrientes 222, Microcentro ☾ noon-4pm & 8:30pm-2am Mon-Fri, 8pm-2am Sat ⊖ Line B, LN Alem ♿ limited, six stairs to enter the building Ⓥ

El Navegante (4, H1)
Argentine $$
A scratched-out menu, yellowing walls, propeller-sized fans, fake hams, dusty framed pictures, faded seafaring murals and gentlemanly waiters all qualify El Navegante as a classic *bodegón*. Avoid the not-quite-fresh seafood and go straight for the standards:

beef, pastas, chicken and tasty *cazuelas* (similar to stews).
☎ 4311-0641 ✉ Viamonte 154, Microcentro ☾ 6am-midnight Mon-Sat ⊖ Line B, LN Alem ♿ good ♠ Ⓥ

Empire Thai (6, E3)
Thai $$$
Tourists and locals alike flock to Empire Thai for classic, *almost* authentic dishes like crispy, wrapped prawns, *panang* chicken (spicy chicken curry) or *tom ka gai* (coconut chicken curry) for lunch. Its outstanding bar (think vodka) and stylish atmosphere up the appeal even more.
☎ 4312-5706 ✉ Tres Sargentos 427, Retiro ☾ noon-1am Mon-Fri, 8pm-1am Sat ☒ 10, 21, 45, 132, 152 & others ♿ good Ⓥ

Filo (6, E3)
Italian $$-$$$
Whether powerlunchers by day or hipsters by night, both slide contentedly into ultra-hip Filo, a superb Italian eatery with a menu as long as the place has been popular. Thin-crust pizza, whopping salads, panini sandwiches, pastas and 18 dessert choices

Seek out Gran Bar Danzón

have dazzled diners for over a decade. Don't miss the art gallery downstairs.
☎ 4311-0312 ✉ www.filo-ristorante.com in Spanish ✉ San Martín 975, Retiro ☾ restaurant noon-4pm & 8pm-2am, pizza all day ⊖ Line C, San Martín ♿ fair Ⓥ

Gran Bar Danzón (6, C2)
International $$$-$$$$
Renowned as much for its wine list as for its food, Gran Bar Danzón sits hidden above its dark, candlelit staircase, spotted only by the scratched-up chalkboard sign sitting on the sidewalk. With some 200 wines to choose from and plenty by the glass, it fills up fast with BA's savviest diners, so arrive early or expect to wait.

Feel the love at Filo

☎ 4811-1108 🖳 www
.granbardanzon.com.ar in
Spanish ✉ Libertad 1161,
Retiro ⏰ 7pm-late, from
8pm Sat & Sun 🚌 10, 39,
67, 102, 152 Ⓥ

Le Sud (6, D1)
French $$$$
For the kind of meal that
sends your eyes rolling in
orgasmic bliss with every
bite, head to the Sofitel's
esteemed Le Sud, where
award-winning chef Thierry
Pszonda (a member of
the Maîtres Cuisiniers de
France) dazzles even the
most refined palates with
exquisitely prepared French
Mediterranean creations.
☎ 4131-0130 ✉ Sofitel,
Arroyo 841, Retiro
⏰ 6:30am-midnight
Ⓜ Line C, San Martín
♿ excellent Ⓥ

Plaza España (4, D4)
Argentine/Italian $$
Though far from fancy,
starting a huge meal off with
a complimentary glass of
moscato (muscat) and ending
with free glass of *limoncello*
(lemon liqueur) makes this
busy joint a pleasurable,
old-time experience. The
menu offers endless choices

of pasta, meat, sandwiches
and more. Great value.
☎ 4383-3271 ✉ Av de
Mayo 1299, Microcentro
⏰ 24hr Ⓜ Line A, Lima
♿ Ⓥ

Sabot (4, G1)
Argentine $$$
The epitome of old-time
porteño eateries, Sabot
means two things: food
and talk. The 24 tables fill
up every weekday, and the
din of business chat fills the
room. Steaks, chicken and
seafood are all good, but
the pastas reign supreme.
Complimentary *limoncello*
and outstanding service.
☎ 4313-6587 ✉ 25 de
Mayo 756, Microcentro
⏰ noon-4pm Mon-Fri
Ⓜ Line B, LN Alem
♿ good Ⓥ

Tancat (6, D3)
Spanish $$$$
With a curving bar, low
ceilings, dimly lit balsa lamps
and intimate seating among
an array of cozy nooks,
Tancat wins on style alone.
Fortunately the food is up to
snuff as well. Platters of real
Spanish ham and *gambas al
ajillo* (garlic prawns) are only
the beginning.

☎ 4312-5442 ✉ Paraguay
645, Retiro ⏰ 12:30-4pm &
8pm-1am Mon-Sat Ⓜ Line
C, San Martín ♿ fair

PUERTO MADERO

Puerto Madero is lined
with high-end restaur-
ants that occupy the
old converted brick
storehouses that line
the waterfront. It's a
great place for lunch
and dinner, but be sure
to choose carefully as
many places are over-
priced. The following
are all excellent.

Bice (4, H1)
Italian $$$$
Parrillas aside, Bice stands
head and shoulders over
most other Puerto Madero
eateries, serving up sublime
Italian food such as black
fettuccini with shrimp,
cloudlike gnocchi and divine
risotto.
☎ 4315-6216 ✉ Av
Alicia Moreau de Justo 192
⏰ noon-4pm & 8pm-1am
Ⓜ Line B, LN Alem Ⓥ ✗

Cabaña Las Lilas (4, J2)
Parrilla $$$$
Buenos Aires' definitive
parrilla serves the city's most
prized steaks, perfectly cut
from the purebred cows that
are fattened up on Cabaña
Las Lilas' private ranch. The
800g, 10cm-thick, baby-beef
steak is as famous as the
wine list, and prices are the
highest in town.
☎ 4313-1336
✉ Av Alicia Moreau de
Justo 516 ⏰ noon-4pm &
7:30pm-midnight Ⓜ Line B,
LN Alem ♿ good ✗

LIKE A BIG PIZZA PIE

Like Chicago and Sicily, Buenos Aires is famous for pizza.
It's either baked *al molde* (similar to deep-dish) or *a la
piedra* (thinner and crispy), and unless you order *fugazza*,
which comes sauceless and smothered in browned onions,
it's loaded with mozzarella. The *fugazzetta* is a *fugazza* with
cheese. A newer invention, and one baked in places like
Morelia (p56) and Filo (p47), is pizza *a la parrilla*, paper-
thin crust topped then cooked on the grill. Mozzarella
slices are traditionally eaten with a slice of *faina* (a thin
chickpea pie) and chased with a glass of *moscato*.

BUSINESS MEALS

If you need a solid business lunch, join the suits at **Sabot** (opposite). **Filo** (p47) is also excellent and conducive to getting the talk in. In Palermo, hit **La Cabrera** (p54), **Bar Uriarte** (p53) or **Olsen** (p55). For dinner, a round of sushi at well-lit **Comedor Nikkai** (p50) is a great choice.

Beats the boardroom – chewing over business at Bar Uriarte

La Caballeriza (4, J3)
Parrilla $$$$
Superb grilled meats and an outrageous gaucho-gone-Las Vegas decor make La Caballeriza a Puerto Madero favorite both for tourists and locals. The dining room is quite an experience, and the outdoor patio makes for great riverside lunches on a sunny afternoon.
☎ 4514-4444 ✉ Av Alicia Moreau de Justo 580 ⏱ noon-4pm & 7:30pm-1am, to 2am Fri & Sat Ⓜ Line B, LN Alem ♿ good ✖

CONGRESO & TRIBUNALES

Bi Won
Korean $$$
From the pickled nibbles, to the hearty *bibimbap* (rice bowl with meat, veggies, egg and hot sauce) to the US$5

bottles of *soju* (a distilled rice beverage), Bi Won serves what's arguably the best Korean food in town. Order the *bulgog* and grill the meat yourself, or singe your palate with the *kimchi* (spicy marinated cabbage) and pork soup. Zing!
☎ 4372-1146 ✉ Junín 548 ⏱ noon-3pm & 7pm-midnight Ⓜ Line B, Pasteur ♿ fair Ⓥ

Chiquilín (4, B3)
Parrilla $$
Chiquilín has been faithfully serving its delicious meats for over 50 years, and the experience shines. Specials like paella on Monday and *puchero* (a meat-and-vegetable stew) on Wednesday add welcome detours to the regular meat menu.
☎ 4373-5163 ✉ Av Sarmiento 1599 ⏱ noon-4pm & 8pm-1am Ⓜ Line B, Uruguay ♿ good ♿

Las Cuartetas (4, E2)
Pizza $
Deemed a cultural heritage site, Las Cuartetas started pumping out its thick-crust (make that *really* thick crust) pizza in the 1920s. Midnight Saturday it's packed with the post-theater and -movie crowd. Order the moz-zarella – anything else might kill you.
☎ 4326-0171 ✉ Av Corrientes 838 ⏱ 11:30am-midnight Mon-Thu, to 2am Fri & Sat, 1am Sun Ⓜ Line B, Carlos Pellegrini; Line C, Diagonal Norte; Line D, 9 de Julio ♿ good ♿ Ⓥ

Laurak Bat (4, D5)
Basque $$
Modest, traditional Laurak Bat is a wonderful place to set your teeth into some genuine Basque food, while marveling the old Guérnica tree brought over from the old country. Seafood

Compliment your meat dish with a bottle of the best at Chiquilín

specialties include *abadejo al pil pil, merluza en salsa verde* (both fish dishes), *cazuela de kokotxas* (fish-cheek stew) and mussels à la Provençal.
☎ 4381-0682 ✉ Av Belgrano 1144 🕑 12:30-3:30pm & 8:30pm-midnight Mon-Sat 🔘 Line A, Lima; Line C, Moreno 🚹 good Ⓥ

Pippo (4, C3)
Parrilla $$
Still going strong after more than 66 years, Pippo whips out reliable *parrilla* and pasta to a happy mix of locals and tourists. With paper tablecloths and a nonsmoking section in the back, it's a happy place to take the kids.
☎ 4375-5887 ✉ Paraná 356 🕑 noon-4pm & 8pm-midnight, to 2am Fri & Sat 🔘 Line B, Uruguay 🚹 good 🚹 Ⓥ ✗

Pizzería Güerrín (4, C2)
Pizza $
A favorite post-theater pizza stop, Güerrín pumps out cheesy slices at about US$0.35 a pop just as fast as folks pour in (and, boy, do they!). Crust is but an afterthought for these mozzarella cheese bombs. Cut the grease with a glass of *moscato*, and

don't forget the *faina* (thin chickpea pie).
☎ 4371-8141 ✉ Av Corrientes 1368 🕑 11am-2am 🔘 Line B, Uruguay 🚹 fair 🚹 Ⓥ

SAN TELMO & LA BOCA

From Japanese cuisine to old-fashioned steak houses, San Telmo's got plenty of choices tucked into the old buildings of its dark and atmospheric streets.

Abril (4, H6)
International $$$
Arguably San Telmo's best upscale restaurant, this small, intimate bistro offers sublime, three-course, prix-fixe dinners in a dimly lit, romantic and totally unpretentious atmosphere. From starters to dessert, the food is exquisite, and the newly added next-door bar is great for a cocktail when you're through.
☎ 4342-8000 ✉ Balcarce 722, San Telmo 🕑 noon-4pm & 8pm-late 🚌 22, 24, 29, 64, 91, 152 & others 🚹 fair

Comedor Nikkai (5, B1)
Japanese $$$
Inside the Japanese Association, Nikkai serves what's likely the city's best sushi – not to mention the many other superb creations gracing the menu. The *combinado* Nikkai plate (US$28), which easily serves three, is a sublime array of *nigiri*, sashimi and *maki* rolls (without an ounce of cream cheese!).
☎ 4300-5848 ✉ Av Independencia 732, San Telmo 🕑 noon-3pm & 7:30-11pm Mon-Thu, noon-3pm & 8pm-midnight Fri, 8pm-midnight Sat 🔘 Line C, Independencia 🚹 fair, three steps to enter 🚹 Ⓥ

Desnivel (5, C1)
Parrilla $
Sure Desnivel is packed with camera-draggers, but it's equally popular with locals. So join in by nudging up to the front-door grill for a *choripan* (sausage sandwich) or by ordering superb grilled meats from the tables. It's dirt cheap, excellent and a BA classic.
☎ 4300-9081 ✉ Defensa 855, San Telmo 🕑 noon-4pm & 8pm-1am 🚌 10, 22, 24, 29, 45 🚹 fair

El Obrero (5, F4)
Parrilla $
The irony of BA's most famous *bodegón* – everyone from Wim Wenders to Robert Duvall and Bono has dined here – is that it's in style without being stylish. It's a Boca classic, with a dusty old atmosphere over 70 years in the making, and pretty much a must-see if you can set aside the Palermo scene. The food (mostly meats and pastas) is good and hardy.
☎ 4362-9912 ✉ Agustín R Caffarena 64, La Boca ☉ noon-midnight Mon-Sat 🚌 29, 64, 86, 152 ♿ fair 🚹

La Brigada (5, B1)
Parrilla $$$
Refined but still oozing old-time atmosphere, La Brigada is arguably San Telmo's best *parrilla*, which explains why, on weekend afternoons, the sidewalk out front is full of salivating locals waiting for their turn to sit down.
☎ 4361-5557 ✉ Estados Unidos 465, San Telmo ☉ noon-4pm & 8pm-midnight 🚌 10, 22, 24, 29, 45 ♿ limited

Manolo (5, B3)
Argentine $
From the dusty football jerseys and photos, to the tie-clad waiters that can

barely squeeze between the wobbly tables, Manolo is a San Telmo institution that shouldn't be missed. The 100-plus items on the menu, from pastas to steaks and *locro* (a hearty grain-and-meat stew), are all dirt cheap. The weekend wait is part of the experience.
☎ 4307-8743 ✉ Bolívar 1502, San Telmo ☉ noon-4pm & 8pm to late 🚌 10, 22, 29, 65, 93 & others ♿ fair, but crowded 🚹 V

Medio y Medio (4, G6)
Sandwiches $
Of the many eateries with outdoor seating on Chile between Defensa and Balcarce, this Uruguayan sandwich shop is a sure shot. *Chivitos* (Uruguayan sandwiches) are all made with beef, pork or chicken, some come with fries and all are massive. *Mate* (traditional Argentine tea) is served with biscuits for US$2.
☎ 4300-7007 ✉ Chile 316, San Telmo ☉ 9am-1am Mon-Thu, 9am Fri-6pm Sun 🚌 2, 9, 22, 24, 45 & others ♿ fair 🚹 V

Origen (5, B2)
Vegetarian $
When it's time to nurture your achin' steak-stomach or to make your meat-eating mate follow *you* for once, head to Origen, a small, friendly

vegetarian eatery complete with outdoor tables. The food is simple and just right, with a few chicken and fish dishes thrown in for carnivores.
☎ 4362-8847 ✉ Perú 1092, San Telmo ☉ noon-4:30pm & 8pm-1am, closed dinner Mon 🚌 10, 20, 22, 29, 45 ♿ fair 🚹 V

Pappa Deus (5, C2)
Italian $$
Pappa Deus shines above the rest of the Plaza Dorrego eateries, serving tasty Italian creations such as pumpkin-filled black ravioli, lamb with roasted peppers, delicious salads and (gosh, out of nowhere) pizza and *parrilla*. Weekdays, tables are dragged out on the plaza.
☎ 4361-2110 ✉ Bethlem 423, San Telmo ☉ 9am-2am 🚌 9, 10, 20, 29, 45 & others ♿ good 🚹 V

Restaurant Lezama (5, C3)
Argentine/Parrilla $-$$
Everyone from neighborhood families to the local priest drop in to dine at parkside Lezama, a San Telmo favorite for over 75 years. The food's honest, the *parrilla* is excellent, and the prices, well…how does a US$4 *bife de chorizo* sound?
☎ 4361-0114 ✉ Brasil 359, San Telmo ☉ noon-4pm & 8pm-2am Mon-Sat,

THE BODEGÓN EXPERIENCE
No visit to Buenos Aires is complete without a visit to the *bodegón*. This is the quintessential porteño restaurant – a traditional, no-frills joint, where food is affordable, waiters are male and character reigns supreme. *Bodegones* have a dusty European feel, have survived the test of time by decades and are rarely without a heavy dose of soccer regalia. The capital's most famous are **El Obrero** (above) and **Desnivel** (opposite), both unforgettable experiences, but perhaps getting a bit too big for their britches. Also try **Manolo** (above), **El Navegante** (p47) and **Restaurant Lezama** (above).

ITALIAN BA

In Buenos Aires, calling Italian food 'Italian' is practically akin to calling hamburgers in the US 'German.' Sure it's Italian, but it's also as Argentine as *parrillas* and gauchos. When over a million Italian immigrants flooded the capital in the late 1800s, they brought their culture of food and wine with them, making pizza and pasta new staples of the porteño diet. Finding fresh, home-style pasta, gelato-like ice cream and countless dishes reminiscent of the boot country is as easy as walking down the block – and they're porteño to the core.

---

noon-5:30pm Sun 🚌 10, 22, 24, 29, 45 & others 🚻 good 🚶

RECOLETA & BARRIO NORTE

Clásica y Moderna (2, B3)
International $$$
Eclectic and old fashioned, this landmark art space, bookstore and restaurant attracts an intellectual crowd for fine food accompanied by excellent live music (usually jazz) and/or poetry readings. It's on the city's list of sites of cultural interest, and with good reason. ☎ 4812-8707 🖳 www .clasicaymoderna.com in Spanish ✉ Rodriguez Peña 835 🕙 8am-1am Mon-Wed, to 3am Fri & Sat 🚇 Line D, Callao 🚻 good Ⓥ

Cumaná (2, B3)
Northern Argentine $
Cumaná dishes out mouth-watering empanadas at US$0.40 a pop, over a dozen delicious *cazuelas* (clay-pot dishes), pizza, calzones and more, all baked in the giant adobe dome oven out back. This is northern Argentine fare at its best: delicious and cheap. Crayons for the kiddos, too.

☎ 4813-9207 ✉ Rodriguez Peña 1149 🕙 noon-midnight Sun-Thu, to 1am Fri & Sat 🚌 10, 12, 21, 39, 152 🚶 Ⓥ

El Sanjuanino (2, C1)
Northern Argentine $
This tiny Recoleta classic is a favorite for traditional Argentine fare such as empanadas, *locro* and other specialties. It's inexpensive, and the owner strolls through on Saturday afternoons shaking hands and mumbling with the customers. ☎ 4805-2683 ✉ Posadas 1515 🕙 noon-4pm & 8pm-late 🚌 17, 62, 92, 93, 130 🚶 Ⓥ

Florencio (2, B1)
Bistro/Bakery $
Skip the Recoleta tourist traps along Junín and sneak off to Florencio, a button-sized café with six marble-top tables, a chalkboard menu, a countertop full of delectable pastries and the perfect selection of sandwiches, salads, crepes, pâté and soup. ☎ 4807-6477 ✉ Francisco de Vittoria 2363 🕙 8am-8pm Mon-Sat 🚌 62, 92, 93 🚶 Ⓥ

Munich Recoleta (2, C2)
International $$
This traditional place hasn't changed much since Borges was a regular; even the waiters seem to be the same. The food (omelets, brochettes, grilled salmon, veggie soup) is consistently good, and the service is prompt. A stand-out on this strip of tourist traps. ☎ 4804-3981 ✉ RM Ortiz 1871 🕙 noon-2am 🚌 17, 62, 67, 92, 93 🚻 good 🚶 Ⓥ

Rigoletto (2, B3)
Italian/International $$
Handsomely classic, Rigoletto is a spick-and-span, checkered-floor bistro with loads on the menu, including pasta, beef, seafood and pizza. ☎ 4313-4777 ✉ Rodriguez Peña 1291 🕙 7am-2am 🚌 10, 12, 21, 152 🚻 good 🚶 Ⓥ

PALERMO

Palermo – especially the sub-neighborhoods Palermo Viejo and Las Cañitas – is easily the city's foodiest neighborhood, and quality is generally high. If you're staying in the Microcentro, it's well worth the short trip out for the evening.

Chueca (7, E6)
International $$$$
Named after the gay district of Madrid, Chueca offers a small menu of tasty dishes such as sesame chicken, grilled chicken in plum sauce, pastas and a spruced-up *ojo*

de bife (rib eye). Reserve a table or you'll be watching the midnight drag show (the real reason to come) from behind a sea of heads.
☎ 4963-3430 ✉ Soler 3283 ☽ 9pm-late Wed-Sat ☒ 29, 92, 109, 128 ♿ limited

Guido's Bar (7, D3)
Italian $$$$
You can't make a wrong choice at eclectic Guido's. In fact, from *antipasti* to *secundi piatti* what you'll eat is entirely up to 'almost honest' chef Carlos, whose Calabrese-influenced food is truly in a class of its own. You're charged depending on how much you eat. Superb.
☎ 4802-2391 ✉ República de la India 2843 ☽ 7am-late Mon-Fri ☒ 10, 37, 60, 64, 67, 152 & others ♿ limited Ⓥ

Pizzería Angelín (7, A5)
Pizza $
Open since 1938, this esteemed old relic still bakes superb pizza. The medium-thick crust has a perfect crunch to the bottom, and cheese is used sensibly. The signature pie is the 'Canchera,' crust and sauce only. Pies and slices are sold.
☎ 4774-3836 ✉ Av Córdoba 5270 ☽ 7pm-midnight, to 2am Fri & Sat ☒ 15, 55, 140, 151, 168 ♿ fair, narrow doorway ♿ Ⓥ

Palermo Viejo
Al Amal (7, A5)
Middle Eastern $$
For a truly divine eating experience, reserve a table (there are only six) at Al Amal. Set aside the menu

and have Lebanese owner and chef Marie Francoise create her own *picada* (small-plates dinner) for you. Hummus, tabouli, stuffed eggplant – she'll know exactly what you need when you walk in the door.
☎ 15-4058-6210 ✉ Godoy Cruz 1601 ☽ 1-3:45pm & 8pm-1am Tue-Sun ☒ 34, 55, 166 Ⓥ

Bar 6 (7, B5)
International $$$
Along with red-velvet couches, chalkboard specials and one of Palermo's longest bars, Bar 6 offers a delectable and manageable menu. Try the *ojo de bife* with mustard sauce. The US$6 set lunch menu is a deal.
☎ 4833-6807 ✉ Armenia 1676 ☽ 8am-late Mon-Sat ☒ 15, 57, 110, 141, 160 ♿ fair Ⓥ

Bar Uriarte (7, B4)
Modern Argentine $$$-$$$$
Chef Guiellermo Testón crafts international cuisine with a nouvelle Argentine flair for savvy diners who drag Palermo shopping bags in by day and wear in what they bought by night. Start with veal carpaccio with fried capers and almonds, continue

with rabbit ravioli, and finish with coconut and lemongrass *panna cotta* (Italian dessert) in a tequila syrup. Gulp.
☎ 4834-6004 ⌨ www.baruriarte.com.ar in Spanish ✉ Uriarte 1572 ☽ noon-4pm & 8pm-1am ☒ 34, 55, 166 ♿ fair Ⓥ ✗

Bereber (7, C5)
Middle Eastern $$$
Mosaic walls, faux snakeskin tablecloths, ambient grooves and exquisitely prepared Moroccan food make Bereber a culinary surety. The tender lamb tagine is superb. Start with one of the creative house cocktails and save room for the flourless chocolate cake. Low tables, divans and obligatory hookahs ice the cake.
☎ 4833-5662 ✉ bereber@dmmdg.com.ar ✉ Armenia 1880 ☽ 8pm-1am ☒ 34, 36, 55, 93, 161 ♿ limited

Bio (7, B3)
Vegetarian $$
All of the food Bio kicks out is organic, vegetarian and delicious. The baked tofu in an orange reduction with salvia and steamed veggies is excellent. The veggie drinks and ginger lemonade will fuel you up too.

Couch or table? Tough decisions at Bar 6.

A MEAL TO REMEMBER

If you're in town on a Friday night, why not join BA's Armenian community for an evening of food, family and fun? **Union General Armenia de Benfecencia** (UGAB; 7, B5; ☎ 4771-6500, 4773-2820; Armenia 1322, Palmero; ☼ 8:30pm-midnight Fri) is a community center and high school that sends its graduating students to Armenia each year. To raise the money, UGAB hosts a huge dinner every Friday night. Students wait tables and their parents prepare traditional Armenian food. There's even a bake sale and a free raffle, and students perform traditional Armenian dances. It's a wonderful family event and a unique chance to experience neighborhood community at its finest. Reservations are required.

☎ 4774-3880 ⊠ Humboldt 2199 ☼ 12:30-4pm Mon, 12:30-4pm & 8pm-midnight Tue-Sun ⊜ 21, 93, 140, 151, 166 ⏾ Ⓥ ✗

Green Bamboo (7, A3)
Vietnamese $$$
Not only do you get superb gourmet Vietnamese food, but also a loungelike Laughing Buddha atmosphere so funky and smooth you might just order another round of dessert (this time, make it the passion-fruit mousse with a chocolate heart). Red booths, Asian kitsch and low-key grooves equal choice dining. ☎ 4775-7050 ⊠ Costa Rica 5802 ☼ 8:30pm-midnight, to 1am Fri & Sat ⊜ 39, 93, 111, 161 ⏾ good Ⓥ

La Cabrera (7, B5)
Argentine/Parrilla $$$
Buenos Aires has more gourmet *parrillas* than you can shake a branding iron at, but this one stands high above the rest, *without* breaking the bank. Don't shy away from the *chinchulines de cordero* (lamb intestines): they're tastier and milder than their bovine equivalent. The *matambre de cerdo* (pork flank) is to die for.

☎ 4831-7002 ⊠ JA Cabrera 5099 ☼ noon-4pm & 8pm-1am Tue-Sun ⊜ 55 ⏾ good

La Dorita (7, B4)
Argentine/Parrilla $$
La Dorita grills up some of the best meat in town, and the excellent prices and casual atmosphere make it one of Palermo's favorites. With traditional *pingüinos* (penguin-shaped wine pitchers) filled from giant wine barrels, wine-bottle lamps and a hilarious rendition of the Last Supper on the wall, it's hard to beat the atmosphere. ☎ 4773-0070 ⊠ Humboldt 1905 ☼ noon-4pm & 8pm-1am ⊜ 21, 111, 161 ⏾ fair

Lelé de Troya (7, B4)
Mediterranean $$-$$$
Duck beneath an overgrown *arbor* and into one of Palermo Viejo's sexiest restaurants, where couples tuck into dark-red corners for cocktails and makeout sessions while diners enjoy fabulous Mediterranean fare in the intimate dining rooms. The wine list is great, the staff is friendly and the rooftop terrace is a summertime must. Come casual or dress to kill.

☎ 4832-2726 ⊠ Costa Rica 4901 ☼ 10am-late ⊜ 34, 55, 166 ⏾ fair Ⓥ

Lomo (7, C5)
Modern Argentine $$$
The essence of Palermo Viejo's trend toward *multiespacios* (multiuse spaces), Lomo is restaurant, record store and art gallery all in one. Unlike some, it succeeds at all three. But the real pull is the food: spruced-up plates of Argentine classics like Patagonian trout, peppered steaks, seafood risotto and succulent sweetbreads. ☎ 4833-3200 ⊠ Costa Rica 4661 ☼ 8:30pm-2am Mon, noon-2am Tue-Sun ⊜ 15, 55 ⏾ good

Maria Fulô (7, B5)
Brazilian $$$
This intimate Brazilian restaurant boasts delectable dishes such as *moqueca de peixe* (fish served with coconut milk, cilantro and seasonings in a clay pot) and

Scandinavian tastes at Olsen

xinxim de galinha (chicken in a shrimp, coconut and cashew sauce). The owner is from São Paulo, which helps explain the superb passion-fruit cocktail *caipirinhas*.
☎ 4831-0103 💻 www .mariafuloresto.com.ar in Spanish ✉ Cabrera 5065 🕑 8pm-2am Mon-Sat 🚌 15, 55, 57, 151, 168 ♿ good

Olsen
Scandinavian $$$-$$$$
Olsen has whipped up a combo that's hard to beat: a lengthy list of vodkas, all kept at exactly 18° below zero; exquisite Scandinavian fare matched only by the equally Scandinavian design; and a lovely, table-filled garden. Swallow that with your venison and roasted quince. The famed Sunday brunch is divine.
☎ 4776-7677 ✉ Gorriti 5870, Palermo Viejo 🕑 noon-1:30am Tue-Sat, 10:30am-8pm Sun 🚌 39, 93, 111, 161 ♿ good Ⓥ 🚫

Te Mataré Ramirez (7, D5)
International $$$
There simply aren't many restaurants with dishes named after sexual positions, and Te Mataré Ramirez (I'll Kill You Ramirez) goes even further: women clad in lingerie act out hilariously vulgar fantasies while sexy male MCs get verbally wild with female diners. It's burlesque at its best, and surprisingly sophisticated. The food? Superb.
☎ 4831-9156 💻 www .tematareramirez.com ✉ Paraguay 4062 🕑 8:30pm-midnight

Sun-Thu, 8:30pm-2am Fri & Sat 🚌 12, 15, 29, 36, 152 & others ♿ fair

Las Cañitas
Bokoto (7, B2)
Sushi $$$
Though you'll have to choose wisely to avoid all the cream cheese, Bakoto is a great spot for sushi. Brick and faux-plastered walls, covered outdoor seating, casual staff and a moody red-and-black decor make for a spellbound evening. Order half-rolls to up the variety.
☎ 4776-6505 💻 www .bokotoresto.com.ar in Spanish ✉ Huergo 261 🕑 8pm-1am 🚌 15, 29, 55, 60, 64 ♿ fair Ⓥ 🚫

El Portugués (7, B2)
Parrilla $$
Garlic braids hang from the corrugated tin ceiling and waiters in T-shirts deliver massive portions of superb grilled meats at one of BA's best and least touristy *parrillas*. You'll likely never see a steak this big again; portions are cut to share.
☎ 4771-8699 ✉ Av Báez 499 🕑 noon-4pm & 8pm-3am 🚌 15, 29, 55, 60, 64 ♿ fair 🚼

Las Cholas (7, B2)
Northern Argentine $-$$
With hearty food, rock-bottom prices and crayons and paper placemats for the kids, Las Cholas is where you join feasting families for

---

I SCREAM, YOU SCREAM
Thanks to its Italian heritage, Argentine *helado* (ice cream) is some of the best in the world. Quintessential flavors are *dulce de leche* (milk caramel) and *dulce de leche granizado* (the same with chocolate flakes) followed closely by *tramontana* (vanilla with caramel swirls and chocolate crispies).

Heladerías (ice-cream parlors) are everywhere, but some stand above the rest. **Freddo** (2, C2; ☎ 0-800-3337-3336; cnr Ayacucho & Av Quintana, Recoleta) and **Persicco** (7, A1; ☎ 0-810-333-7377, cnr Maure & Migeletes, Las Cañitas) are excellent. **Munchi's** (6, D3; ☎ 0-800-555-5050, cnr MT de Alvear & Florida, Retiro) is even creamier and **Un Altra Volta** (7, E3; ☎ 4805-1818, Av del Libertador 3060, Palermo) is arguably the best. All have other branches.

Space to sit and lick at Un Altra Volta

KEEPING THE VEGGIE FAITH

Staying vegetarian in carnivore country is surprisingly easy. Pasta, of course, is everywhere (even most *parrillas* have it on the menu), and pizza is prolific. Japanese restaurants like **Comedor Nikkai** (p50) have excellent meatless meals, as do the **Chinese restaurants** in Belgrano. **Cumaná** (p52) serves all sorts of veggie items that still offer a true taste of northwest Argentina. Also treat yourself to **Bio** (p53) and **Florencio** (p52).

---

delicious empanadas, veggies and pizza all pulled from the giant domed adobe oven out back. Steaks, tamales, *humitas* (steamed cornmeal wrapped in corn husks), sandwiches and *mate* are on offer too.
☎ 4899-0094 ✉ Arce 306 ☽ noon-1am Mon-Thu, noon-2am Fri-Sun 🚌 15, 29, 55, 64, 118 ♿ good 🍴 Ⓥ

Morelia (7, B2)
Italian $$
Layering gourmet toppings onto a paper-thin crust and cooking it *a la parrilla* (on the grill), Morelia redefines pizza – just as you'll redefine your idea of what makes a great pie. This stuff is truly sublime. The atmosphere is hip without being pretentious, with dim lighting enhanced by low, bass-heavy grooves.
☎ 4772-0329 ✉ Av Báez 260 ☽ 8pm-1am 🚌 15, 29, 55, 60, 64 Ⓥ

BELGRANO & COLEGIALES

Buddha BA (3, A2)
Asian $$$
An outpost of cool in BA's China Town, Buddha BA serves some of the city's finest pan-Asian cuisine, offering a small menu of Thai and Chinese fusion dishes

and a melt-into-your-chair atmosphere. Funky chandeliers, an Asian art gallery and an orchid room make it even more inviting.
☎ 4706-2382 🖵 www .buddhaba.com.ar in Spanish ✉ Arribeños 2288, Belgrano ☽ 12:30-3pm & 8:30pm-midnight Tue-Sun 🚌 15, 29, 60, 64, 118 & others ♿ fair Ⓥ

Contigo Peru (3, A3)
Peruvian $-$$
Top off a plate of cheap Peruvian ceviche (raw seafood 'cooked' in lemon juice) with a *pisco sour* (imagine a Peruvian margarita) or some neon-pink Inka Kola.
☎ 4780-3960 🖵 www .contigo-peru.com.ar in Spanish ✉ Echeverría 1627, Belgrano ☽ 11am-midnight Tue-Sun 🚌 15, 29, 60, 64, 118 ♿ fair 🍴

Siempre Verde (3, A3)
Chinese/Vegetarian $
This small family-run eatery serves up delicious vegetarian food at bargain prices. It's a little heavy on the rice and noodle dishes, but still a great break from meat.
☎ 15-5454-6481 ✉ Arribeños 2127, Belgrano ☽ noon-4pm & 7-11pm Mon-Fri, noon-11pm Sat & Sun 🚌 15, 29, 60, 64, 118 & others ♿ limited 🍴 Ⓥ ✗

Sifones & Dragones
International $$$
For something completely different try Sifones & Dragones, 'Not a restaurant,' as the card says, 'but a kitchen with tables.' With mismatched furniture, imaginative dishes like chicken in blackberry curry, and a carnivalesque sound track, it's like joining Sgt Pepper for a trip down the rabbit hole. With seven tables, reservations are a must.
☎ 15-4413-9871 🖵 www.sifonesydragones .com.ar in Spanish ✉ Ciudad de La Paz 174, Colegiales ☽ 9pm-12:30am Tue-Thu, 8:30pm-1:30am Fri & Sat 🚌 39, 68, 152 ♿ good Ⓥ

Todos Contentos (3, A3)
Chinese $$
For those who find noodle soups and an ice-cold beer the perfect hangover cure, welcome to postparty paradise. The rest of the lengthy but standard menu (sweet-and-sour, chow mein, *kung pao* etc) is quite good, and vegetarians have plenty of choice, but the soups make it shine.
☎ 4780-3437 ✉ Arribeños 2177, Belgrano ☽ 11:30am-4pm & 8-11:30pm Mon-Sat, 11:30am-midnight Sun 🚌 15, 29, 60, 64, 118 & others ♿ fair 🍴 Ⓥ

Entertainment

Start your mantras now: 'Life is too short to sleep; the night is too young to stop.' Only after drilling these simple new realities into your head will you be able to keep up with porteños (BA residents). Remember, this is a city that doesn't even *eat* until after 10pm. And age is not a factor. You'll hardly be the first foreigner holding your head up at a *milonga* (tango dance hall) while dancers old enough to put *you* to bed are only just getting their second wind.

A good night out works like this: dinner and conversation until midnight, off to a bar for a little fuel, followed by a *boliche* (smaller dance venue or bar) and finally, some time after 2am, the *discoteca* (dance club).

If staying awake past midnight is beyond your ability, no worries. Live music often starts around 10pm, and theatrical performances begin as early as 8pm. You'll just have to eat dinner afterwards and roll off to bed with a full stomach. Many tango shows are presented over dinner, which means you'll still be free, for bed or for more, by midnight.

Whether it's tango lessons, bars, theaters, movies or clubs you're after, there's something to do every night of the week. To find out what, where and when, pick up copies of the free entertainment weeklies *Llegás* and *Cultura BA* (both available at tourist offices), or consult the Friday edition of the *Buenos Aires Herald,* which has its weekly entertainment section called 'Get Out!'. Online, check out www.whatsupbuenosaires.com for all types of entertainment. For nightclubs see www.buenosaliens.com (in Spanish). For listings of nearly every *milonga* in the capital, see www.buenosairesmilongas.com. Tickets to performances at larger venues are sold through **Ticketek** (7, E5; ☎ 5237-7200; www.ticketek.com.ar in Spanish; Alto Palermo, Av Santa Fe 3253), which has outlets through the city.

CAFÉS

One of the greatest joys of visiting Buenos Aires is hanging out in its cafés. They're integral to life in Buenos Aires, and few porteños make it through the day without popping into one for an afternoon *cortado* (espresso cut with milk). The following are some of the city's best and most historic.

Café Paulin (4, F3)
While pedestrians are doing the shoulder-slam along Florida, slip off the drag and into this narrow café. Order a *cortado* (akin here to a minilatte) and watch your head slip into infinity in the mirrored walls on both sides of the center bar.
☎ 4325-2280
✉ Sarmiento 635, Microcentro ⏰ 6am-9pm Mon-Sat 🚇 Line B, Florida; Line C, Diagonal Norte; Line D, 9 de Julio

Richmond (4, F2)
If there's one café on Florida you don't want to miss, this is it. The Richmond café has been serving up giant afternoon teas (complete with four kinds of pastries) since 1917, and the giant red chairs make it tough to haul your full belly away from the table. In the smoky den downstairs, men play chess, checkers, backgammon and pool.
☎ 4322-1341 🖥 www .restaurant.com.ar/rich mond in Spanish ✉ Florida 468, Microcentro ⏰ 7am-10pm Mon-Sat 🚇 Line B, Florida; Line C, Lavalle ♿ fair 🚻

Café royalty

SPECIAL EVENTS

Many of BA's biggest events take place at Palermo's giant convention center, **Predio La Rural** (7, C3; Av Santa Fe 4201).

February *Carnaval* – it ain't Río, but it's fun. A recent lift on the water-balloon ban means the streets are livelier and, as always, the *murga* (traditional Carnaval drummers and dancers) groups drive the crowd wild. Dates vary.

February/March *Buenos Aires Tango* (www.tangodata.com.ar) – BA's weeklong tango festival, with *milongas,* shows and street performances throughout the city, is not one to miss.

March *Exposición de Caballos Criollos* (www.caballoscriollos.com in Spanish) – late March; expo at Predio La Rural showcasing the hardy Argentine criollo breeds that were traditionally used by the gauchos.

April *Festival Internacional de Cine Independiente* (www.bafici.gov.ar) – mid- to late April; BA's citywide independent film fest.

April/May *Feria del Libro* (www.el-libro.com.ar in Spanish) – BA's annual book fair for three weeks at Predio La Rural.

May *arteBA* (www.arteba.com) – mid-May; practically worth planning a trip around, this huge contemporary art fair at Predia La Rural is the biggest of its kind in Latin America.

July/August *La Rural* (www.ruralarg.org.ar in Spanish)– Argentina's most important livestock fair, with cows, pigs, sheep, bulls, horses and, best of all, gaucho competitions. Held at Predia La Rural.

August/September *Fashion BA* – huge fashion-design fair at Predia La Rural.

September *La Semana de Arte en Buenos Aires* (www.lasemanadelarte.com.ar in Spanish)– mid-September; five cultural centers, 25 museums and some 100 art galleries highlight Argentina's best contemporary artists.

October *Festival Guitarras del Mundo* (www.festivaldeguitarras.com.ar in Spanish) – guitarists descend on BA to play everything from jazz to tango and folk.

November *Marcha del Orgullo Gay* (www.marchadelorgullo.org.ar in Spanish) – first Saturday; thousands of gay, lesbian and transgender participants march from Plaza de Mayo to the Congreso. Gay Pride week follows later in November.

Día de la Tradición – mid-November; nationwide celebration of gaucho culture. Best places to be are the Feria de Mataderos (p15) or San Antonio de Areco (p35).

Creamfields – huge outdoor rave held behind Puerto Madero on varying dates in November.

December *Campeonato Abierto Argentino de Polo* – one of the world's most important polo championships takes places at Palermo's Campo Argentino de Polo (p68).

Laboring over an open-air grill during Feria de Mataderos

Café Tortoni (4, E4)

So what if half the clientele is fresh off the tourist bus and the cappuccinos are over-priced? This landmark café is – Tortoni claims – the oldest café in the country. Opened in 1858, everything from the hardwood columns and stained-glass ceilings of the main hall, to the giant porcelain-and-copper urinals in the men's room, oozes history.

☎ 4342-4328 ✉ Av de Mayo 829, Microcentro ☽ 7:30am-2am Mon-Sat, 9am-1am Sun ⊕ Line C, Av de Mayo; Line A, Piedras ♿ fair

El Federal (5, B1)

Skip the touristy cafés around Plaza Dorrego and head two blocks northwest to El Federal, which has been serving up coffee and booze since 1864. The arched bar is one of the most beautiful you'll set eyes on, and behind it, the floor is lowered so the barmen can see eye-to-eye with seated drinkers.

☎ 4300-4313 ✉ cnr Perú y Carlos Calvo, San Telmo ☽ 7:30am-1:30am Sun-Thu, to 3am Fri & Sat ▣ 10, 20, 29, 45, 86 & others ♿ fair

History on the walls of Café Tortoni

La Biela (2, C2)

One of Jorge Luis Borges' favorite cafés, this landmark café is synonymous with the 1960s literary scene, with Recoleta's upper echelons and with the enormous rubber tree whose branches hang over the outdoor patio. It's well worth popping in for a coffee after a jaunt through the cemetery.

☎ 4804-0449 ▢ www .labiela.com ✉ Av Quintana 596, Recoleta ☽ 7am-3am ▣ 10, 21, 59, 60, 93 ♿ excellent

La Puerto Rico (4, G4)

Originally located on Perú, La Puerto Rico opened in 1887 and moved to this location in 1928. Within BA's café hierarchy it's second only to Café Tortoni, yet its fresh ground coffee is second to none.

☎ 4331-2215 ▢ www .lapuertoricocafé.com.ar in Spanish ✉ Adolfo Alsina 416, Monserrat ☽ 7am-8pm Mon-Fri, 7am-4pm Sat ⊕ Line A, Plaza de Mayo; Line E, Bolivar ♿ fair

Las Violetas (3, C2)

While Café Tortoni is dark, brooding and masculine, Las Violetas is bright, cheerful and, well, full of women. For over 120 years Las Violetas has been turning out the city's most famous *facturas* (pastries), which you can stuff down beneath marble columns and giant stained-glass windows as white-jacketed waiters slip among a mostly local clientele.

☎ 4958-7387 ▢ www .lasvioletas.com in Spanish ✉ Rivadavia 3899, Almagro ☽ 6am-1am Mon-Thu, 6am-4am Fri & 6am Sat-1am Sun ⊕ Line A, Castro Barros ♿ good

WHAT'S YOUR POISON?

Imports are expensive, so tone down your taste buds and go for the local swills: Quilmes is the number one beer, but Isenbeck and Warsteiner are close behind and better. Order a *porrón* and you'll get a bottle, a *chopp* and you'll get a frosty mug of draught. Twenty-somethings love Fernet with Coke, a medicinal tasting mix guaranteed to induce a painful hangover (remember, the first one always sucks). New Age, a sparkling wine, is all the rage among the ladies. Gancia, a locally produced Italian aperitif, hurts by itself but when whipped up with soda and lemon makes a divine summertime drink called Gancia Batido.

BARS

Sink a few in Deep Blue

Acabar (7, A4)

Check your cool at the door, grab a board game off the shelf and join the wackiness. With corrugated tin slapped on the walls, crystal chandeliers, leopard-print mannequins, multicolored pots and pans and over 100 mismatched tables, the vibe is pure *fun*. The effect of house music on the revelry is perfect. ☎ 4772-0845 ✉ Honduras 5733, Palermo Hollywood ☽ 8pm-2am Sun-Thu, 8pm-4:30am Fri & Sat ☒ 39, 93, 111, 161 ♿ limited ♨

Buller Brewing Company (2, C2)

Stainless-steel tanks above the bar immediately make clear the priority here: micro-brewed beer. You get properly poured imperial pints too, so enjoy 'em while you can. ☎ 4808-9061 ✉ RM Ortiz 1827, Recoleta ☽ noon-late ☒ 17, 61, 62, 93, 110 ♿ good ♨ during lunch

Deep Blue (2, B2)

This futuristic tavern is blue all right, from the glowing bar top to the industrial, corrugated-tin walls to the mood lighting that even gives fake-tanned skin a blue cast. It could have been in *Blade-runner* if not for the pool tables, the big-screen TV and the darn good snack menu that keep you anchored in the present. ☎ 4827-4415 ✉ Ayacucho 1240, Recoleta ☽ 6pm-3am Sun-Thu, to 6am Fri & Sat ☒ 10, 21, 39, 152 ♿ good

Doctor Mason (7, B6)

It's all about the beer here: Argentine microbrews by Cervecería El Bolsón and Cervecería Blest, plus Guinness, Duvel, bocks, stouts and pils, both bottled and pulled. The dark, publike atmosphere is excellent, there are pool tables downstairs and the kitchen serves exquisitely presented, imaginative meals. ☎ 4777-7889 ⌨ www.doctormason.com.ar in Spanish ✉ Aráoz 1199, Palermo Viejo ☽ noon-late ☒ 15, 55, 57 ♿ fair on ground floor

El Verde (6, E3)

The truly odd cast of characters that inhabits El Verde keep the party crowd faithful to the *other* bars on the street, making this the one where you can actually have a low-decibel chat. Salty peanuts, mounted animal heads and gentle old bartenders – hey, where's Bukowski? ☎ 4315-3693 ✉ Reconquista 878, Retiro ☽ noon-5am ⊖ Line C, San Martín ♿ fair

Fin del Mundo (4, G6)

A good spot to kick off a night in San Telmo, little

City essentials 1A: popular Irish pub? Tick.

Fin del Mundo steers clear of the electronica music, firing out nonstop classics instead, from the Stones to Os Mutantes.

✉ cnr Defensa & Chile, San Telmo ⏰ 6pm-3am 🚌 10, 26, 29, 45, 86 ♿ fair

Gibraltar (5, B1)
A motley mix of expats and Argentines crowd this friendly pub, milling around the pool table out back, draining pints at the bar or chin-wagging around the wobbly tables in front.

☎ 4362-5310 ✉ Perú 895, San Telmo ⏰ 6pm-4am Mon-Thu, 6pm-6am Fri & Sat, 12:30pm-4am Sun Ⓜ Line C, Independencia ♿ fair

Kilkenny (6, E2)
The cornerstone of the seedy strip of bars along the 900 block of Reconquista, Kilkenny packs 'em in nightly. Guinness and Van Morrison come as no surprise, while the dungeonesque feel, giant smoking hearth and carved gnome heads ghoulishly complement the party vibe.

☎ 4312-7291 ✉ MT de Alvear 399, Retiro ⏰ 6pm-6am Mon-Fri, 8pm-6am Sat & Sun Ⓜ Line C, San Martín

La Farmacia (5, B1)
Tuck into one of several dimly lit rooms for an evening of bossa nova and smooth ambient grooves, or slip up to the plant-filled rooftop terrace in summer. The deep red walls and casual atmosphere make this a tough spot to leave. There's a good dinner and snack menu too.

☎ 4300-6151 🖥 www .lafarmaciarestobar.com.ar in Spanish ✉ Bolívar 898,

A motto to remember (while you can)

San Telmo ⏰ 10am-2am Tue-Sun 🚌 10, 22, 24, 29, 45 ♿ fair, front room only

Milión (6, B3)
Never partied in a mansion? Here's your chance. With superb art, a living-room DJ, and three floors of converted rooms, Milión is a nighttime Never Never Land. Feast on nouvelle Argentine cuisine in the dining room, chill out on the terrace, explore the bedrooms or follow the giant marble staircase to the gardens out back.

☎ 4815-9925 🖥 www .milion.com.ar ✉ Paraná 1048, Barrio Norte ⏰ noon-2am Mon-Wed, noon-3am Thu, noon-4am Fri, 8pm-4am Sat, 8pm-2am Sun 🚌 10, 29, 39, 152 ♿ fair, ground floor only

Mundo Bizarro (7, C4)
As if potent cocktails, comfy booths, Tex-Mex food and a giant psychedelic bug weren't enough, they had to add a foot stompin', finger pickin', rockabilly sound track too (and we're not talkin' the oldies-but-goodies mom used to like).

☎ 4773-1967 ✉ Guatemala 4802, Palermo Viejo ⏰ 8pm-3am

Sun-Wed, 8pm-4am Thu, 8pm-5am Fri & Sat Ⓜ Line D, Plaza Italia ♿ fair

Unico (7, A4)
Is it the Heineken and Camel ads, the infectious pop music, the giant fruit cocktails or the cramped quarters that spell 'pickup scene'? Either way, you might get lucky here.

☎ 4775-6693 ✉ Honduras 5604, Palermo Hollywood ⏰ 9am-4am Sun-Thu, to 6am Fri & Sat 🚌 39, 93, 111, 161

LIVE MUSIC

Club del Vino (7, B5)
Wine and music – what more could you want? Reservations. Yep, call ahead if you want a downstairs table (although upstairs-front is far more intimate). A music hall-cum-wine bar with seating for 200, Club del Vino packs in the upscale crowd for top-notch tango and jazz, accompanied by an excellent wine list and whopping cheese platters.

☎ 4833-0048/0049 ✉ JA Cabrera 4737, Palermo Viejo 💲 US$4-10 ⏰ from 9:30pm Wed-Sun 🚌 15, 55, 57, 140, 168 ♿ good ✖

Music, wine and alfresco romance at Club del Vino (p61)

La Peña del Colorado
(7, E5)

For live *folkórica* (folk music) nearly every night of the week, reserve a table at Peña del Colorado, one of the best *peñas* (folk venues) in the city. There's a delicious *parrilla* (grill restaurant) and Northern Argentine foods are served (though not required), and there's *mate* (traditional Argentine tea) too. Music starts at 10pm.
☎ 4822-1038 ▯ www .lapeniadelcolorado.com.ar ✉ Güemes 3657, Palermo 💲 US$2.50-5 🕑 11am-2am

Sun-Thu, to 3am Fri & Sat 🚇 Line D, Bulnes ♿ good

La Trastienda (4, G5)
From tango to rock and roll, La Trastienda is the smallest of Buenos Aires' 'major venues' (it was once a mansion, after all) and hosts some of the country's finest musicians as well as international acts, including Café Tacuba, Compay Segundo, Yo La Tengo and Stereolab. The stage is low, and the floor holds about 1000 standing plus another 350 in seats above.

☎ 4342-7650 ▯ www .latrastienda.com in Spanish ✉ Balcarce 460, San Telmo 💲 US$1.50-5 🕑 from 9pm Wed-Sun 🚌 10, 20, 24, 45, 86 ♿ good

Luna Park (4, H2)
Luna Park is possibly one of BA's most historic and important performance venues, and turning up for a show at this neon-signed classic is quite an experience. Formerly a sports hall, it now hosts everything from rock and roll to *Disney on Ice* in its vast, unadorned interior. Juan and Eva Perón met here.
☎ 4324-1010 ▯ www .lunapark.com.ar in Spanish ✉ cnr Bouchard & Av Corrientes, Microcentro 💲 US$3-30 🕑 varies 🚇 Line B, LN Alem ♿ limited, depends on event 👶 depends on event

A FINE TIME FOR WINE

Wine lovers, welcome to heaven. Almost overnight Argentina has gone from a producer of unexceptional wine consumed by the local market to a respected exporter of outstanding varietals (also embraced by locals). Argentina's main wine regions are Mendoza and San Juan, but everything makes its way to Buenos Aires, where you can pick up an excellent bottle for as little as US$5.

Malbec, Argentina's signature red, is a wine whose subtle and wonderfully drinkable characteristics have been nurtured with success only in Argentina. San Juan produces excellent *syrahs,* as well as *torrontés,* a lovely dry white wine also unique to Argentina. Numerous other varietals and blends (particularly cabernet/*malbec*) have all done exceptionally well. And the vast number of boutique wineries popping up means you could spend your entire trip sampling different labels without even scratching the surface.

Catena Zapata is widely considered Argentina's best winery. Saint Felicien and Alamos are Catena's lower-priced national labels and are excellent for their prices. Luigi Bosca produces superb wines; its Finca La Linda label gets you similar Luigi Bosca quality at half the price. For a unique treat pick up a bottle of Patagonian winery Humberto Canale's Marcus Gran Reserva *malbec.* Other esteemed wineries include Felipe Rutini, Nieto Senetiner, Monchenot and Fabre Montmayou. For good, midrange buys (in the US$4 to US$6 range) try Finca Flichman, Terrazas, Navarro Correas and Trapiche.

N/D Ateneo (6, C3)
When you're combing the papers' music listings, pay close attention to this one. N/D Ateneo hosts excellent musicians from all genres. It's a remodeled theater and the atmosphere is hard to beat.
☎ 4328-2888 ⊠ Paraguay 918, Retiro ⑤ US$4-10 ☼ box office noon-8pm Mon-Sat, closed Jan ♿ good

Notorious (2, B3)
It's hard to go wrong at Notorious, one of BA's premier jazz venues, thanks to its intimacy, multigenerational crowd and superb nightly performances. There's not a bad seat in the house, but definitely reserve a table to get up close. Dinner, drinks and desserts are optional at an additional, reasonable charge.
☎ 4813-6888, 4815-8473 ▯ www.notoriousbar.com.ar in Spanish ⊠ Av Callao 966, Recoleta ⑤ US$3-7 ☼ from 9pm ◉ Line D, Callao ♿ good

DANCE CLUBS

Asia de Cuba (4, J3)
Fuel up on a plate of the house sushi (which will also clear you of Asia's cover charge)

PEÑAS & FOLKLÓRICA
It only takes two to tango, but it takes 20 to dance the *chacarera*. And the same to dance the *chamamé*, the *samba* (not the Brazilian samba, but the Argentine *samba*) and the *carnavalito*. These are Argentina's folk dances, rhythms that are easy to miss in the city of tango, tango, tango. They're equally captivating and easier to learn, and everyone dances them together in a big happy line dance. *Peñas* (folk venues) are the best places to hear *folklórica* (folk music), and the best *peña* in town is La Peña del Colorado (p62).

before hitting the packed dance floor; the mix of eclectic dance music, sweaty bodies and scantily clad female show dancers have a way of keeping you cheering and dancing until the sun comes up.
☎ 4894-1328 ⊠ Dealessi 750, Puerto Madero Este ⑤ US$11 ☼ restaurant 9pm-1am daily, club from 1am Tue-Sat ▣ 20, 33, 56, 64, 152 & others

Basement (2, B3)
Deep down inside (or rather, under) Recoleta's Shamrock Bar, the Basement club is a sure shot for a good night, pulling in an even mix of expats and locals for the barrage of house music that keeps 'em spilling their sweat all over the small dance floor well into the night.

☎ 4812-3584 ▯ www.theshamrockbar.com ⊠ Rodríguez Peña 1220, Recoleta ⑤ bar free, club US$2 ☼ club hours from midnight, 1am or 2am, depending on event ▣ 10, 21, 37, 101, 152

Club Niceto (7, A4)
Niceto's Thursday night Club 69, complete with outrageous drag shows and heaving house music, has been pulling in the faithful for years. Unfortunately it's often too packed to move (let alone dance) so you'll either have to push through to the wee hours when the floor thins out, or drop in on Saturday when it's less crowded.
☎ 4779-9396 ⊠ Niceto Vega 5510, Palermo ⑤ US$3-5 ☼ from 2am Thu-Sat ▣ 21, 93, 111, 151, 168

Cocoliche (4, E4)
Whether the minister of sound is a whacked-out band or one of BA's best DJs (and the latter is often the case), you're pretty much guaranteed a good time and a good crowd at this electronica paradise based in a converted mansion.
☎ 4331-6413 ⊠ Av Rivadavia 878, Microcentro

Enjoy the calm before dancing a storm at Asia de Cuba

($) US$2-5 (time) midnight-late Fri & Sat (subway) Line A, Piedras

El Living (6, B3)
At 10 years old, El Living is ancient but still going strong, thanks to its small floor, central location and the fun mix of Latin pop, '80s mod and house. Dinner is served from 10pm to 12:30am, and when the dining's done, the back room is cleared for dancing. Doors closed to nondiners until 1am.
(phone) 4811-4730 (mail) MT del Alvear 1540, Retiro ($) free with dinner; US$2 after 1am (time) 10pm-6am Thu-Sat (bus) 10, 21, 39, 102, 152

Maluco Beleza (4, B3)
Slip into something more tropical and drop into Maluco Beleza, a two-level Brazilian *boliche* where samba, live music, show dancers and a sprinkling of cheesy 1980s pop tunes are all guaranteed to lift your spirits. Upstairs, house and techno pound through several rooms of happy dancers. There are dinner shows on Wednesday and Saturday at 10pm.
(phone) 4372-1737 (computer) www .malucobeleza.com.ar in Spanish (mail) Sarmiento 1728, Microcentro ($) US$4 (time) club from 1am Wed & Fri-Sun (subway) Line B, Callao

Pachá
Buenos Aires' version of Ibiza's famed Pachá is a cornerstone of the capital's club scene, and Saturday night's Clubland is unforgettable. A frenzied night of hedonistic boogying until the sun rises over this riverfront terrace is not to be missed.

NIGHTCLUB SAFETY CODES
On December 30, 2004, the República Cromañón nightclub in the barrio of Once caught fire, killing 194 people in what was soon deemed Argentina's worst non-natural disaster. Following the fire, all nightclubs in BA were shut down and remained closed until inspected by officials. Most of the nightclubs listed here have reopened (or were planning to), though some will only operate as bars until procuring a new dance license. To find out what's open, contact the tourist offices (see p90). Safety codes have been strictly enforced since the tragedy.

(phone) 4788-4280 (mail) cnr Av Costanera Rafael Obligado & La Pampa, Costanera Norte (time) Fri & Sat Feb-Dec (bus) 28, 42, 107, 130, 160

THEATER

Centro Cultural de la Cooperación (4, B2)
Another major Corrientes venue, this centre hosts everything from theater, dance and music to documentary films, literary events and children's shows.
(phone) 5077-8000 (computer) www .cculturalcoop.org.ar in Spanish (mail) Av Corrientes 1543, Tribunales ($) US$2-12 (time) box office 5-10pm Wed & Thu, 5pm-midnight Fri, 1:30pm-midnight Sat, 1:30-9pm Sun; cultural center 9am-10pm Mon-Fri, 1:30pm-10pm Sat & Sun (subway) Line B, Uruguay (access) excellent (children) children's shows

Teatro Astral (4, B2)
From highly produced tango productions such as Diego Romay's *Tanguera* to over-the-top musicals, Teatro Astral is a great place for non-Spanish speakers to catch a show that's high

on spectacle and low on language.
(phone) 4374-5707/9964 (mail) Av Corrientes 1639, Tribunales ($) US$5-15 (time) box office 10am-10pm (subway) Line B, Uruguay (access) good (children) children's shows

Teatro La Plaza (4, B3)
Part of Paseo La Plaza – which has boutique shops, a café with outdoor seating, bars and even a tattoo parlor – Teatro La Plaza is by far the most commercial venue of Corrientes' cultural centers. Productions run the gamut from classic to contemporary.
(phone) 6320-5300 (mail) Av Corrientes 1660, Tribunales ($) US$3-12 (time) box office 10am-8pm Mon-Wed, to 11pm Thu-Sun (subway) Line B, Callao (access) good (children) children's shows

Teatro Nacional Cervantes (4, D1)
Although it's showing its 85-plus years, the Cervantes is an architectural gem, presenting theater, comedy, musicals and dance in any of its three gorgeous halls. The grand lobby and red-velvet chairs make it quite a treat.

☎ 4816-4224 ⌨ www
.teatrocervantes.gov.ar in
Spanish ✉ Libertad 815,
Tribunales 💲 US$2-6
☷ box office 10am-8pm,
closed Jan ⊕ Line D,
Tribunales ♿ good
♿ children's shows

Teatro San Martín (4, B2)
Corrientes' premier theater
houses three auditoriums
with productions ranging
from dance and theater to
children's shows. There are
often excellent (and free)
photography exhibits in the
lobby. Teatros Alvear, Regio,
de la Ribera and Sarmiento
all pertain to San Martín;
pick up a program for any of
these and purchase tickets
here.
☎ 0-800-333-5254
⌨ www.teatrosanmartin
.com.ar ✉ Av Corrientes
1530, Tribunales 💲 US$1-5
☷ box office 10am-10pm
⊕ Line B, Uruguay ♿ fair
♿ children's shows

TANGO

Tango Shows
Bar Sur (5, C1)
Not only is Bar Sur one of BA's
most intimate places for a
tango dinner show (complete
with live music and only a
dozen tables), but the bar
itself is a masterpiece of
nostalgia. It just *feels* cool.
Plus, the price is better than
at bigger venues, and the
staff is great. Reservations
are a must.
☎ 4362-6086 ⌨ www
.bar-sur.com.ar ✉ Estados
Unidos 299, San Telmo
💲 dinner show US$30
☷ 8pm-3am 🚌 10, 22, 29,
86, 126 & others

El Balcón (5, C2)
If you can't take the steep
prices and overproduction
of other tango shows, head
upstairs to El Balcón, where
having a good time is all
that really matters. No *fixed*
menu, but you are required
to eat, and the show is
included. Reservations are
advised, especially on Sunday
afternoons.
☎ 4362-2354 ✉ 1st fl,
Humberto 1° 461, San Telmo
💲 meals US$3-8 ☷ shows
10pm Fri & Sat, 1:30-7pm
Sun; lunch & dinner Tue-Sun
🚌 10, 20, 22, 24, 45 ♿

El Querandí (4, F5)
'Dinner show' is an under-
statement. The nightly shows
at El Querandí are tango
extravaganzas, with live
music and swirling dancers
ripping up a big stage while
formal waiters in striped
shirts and bowties deliver
food to the tourists. The
dining room is exquisite.
☎ 4345-1770 ⌨ www
.querandi.com.ar in Spanish
✉ Perú 302, Monserrat
💲 dinner show US$57
☷ 12:30-4pm, dinner show
8:30pm-late ⊕ Line E,
Bolívar ♿ fair

El Viejo Almacén (5, C1)
Since 1969 some of the city's
best tango singers, dancers
and musicians have been
performing at this highly
regarded venue. It's definitely
one of the more atmospheric
spots to catch a show.
☎ 4307-7388 ⌨ www
.viejoalmacen.com ✉ cnr
Balcarce & Independencia,
San Telmo 💲 show US$35,
dinner & show US$50 ☷ din-
ner from 8pm, show 10pm
🚌 10, 20, 22, 24, 45 ♿ good

Señor Tango
This is the closest you'll get to
Las Vegas in BA's tango world,
and, with live horses involved,
it's definitely the most outrageous. If you like spectacle,
you'll like Señor Tango.
☎ 4303-0231 ⌨ www
.senortango.com.ar in
Spanish ✉ Vieytes 1655,
Barracas 💲 show & dinner
US$55, show only US$35
🚌 12, 20, 45, 70, 134 ♿ fair

Tango Lessons & Milongas
Academia Nacional del Tango (4, E4)
Located above the historic
Café Tortoni, the National

PLAYIN' THE LONER
Porteños are relentlessly curious about foreigners, and
going out alone can easily lead to a friendly evening
of Spanglish and miming. Weeknights are mellow and
friendly at Palermo's **Mundo Bizarro** (p61). If you just
want to chat with fellow foreigners, hit **Gibraltar** (p61)
in San Telmo. Don't rule out dancing tango – **milongas**
often start with group lessons and partners get swapped.
Live music can be better alone than with a chatty mate,
so hit **Notorious** (p63) or **N/D Ateneo** (p63). An opera
at the **Teatro Colón** (p17) is definitely romantic, but
with music like this who needs distractions?

Academy of Tango is an excellent resource for information on classes and *milongas* throughout the city. Lessons, of course, are also offered.
☎ 4345-6967 ☐ www .anacdeltango.org.ar in Spanish ✉ Av de Mayo 833, Microcentro $ US$1-5 ☾ 10am-8pm Mon-Fri ⊙ Line A, Piedras

Centro Cultural Torquato Tasso (5, C3)
Whether you come for the superb tango musicians that regularly take to the stage, for the classes that precede every dance, or just to watch the *milongueros* (dancers) do their thing, CC Torquato Tasso won't let you down. It's a popular, lively place with plenty of tables and outstanding performances.
☎ 4307-6506 ✉ Defensa 1575, San Telmo $ US$2-5 ☾ from 8pm or 10pm Fri-Sun ⊟ 10, 22, 45, 64, 71

Confitería Ideal (4, E2)
Although incense wafts among the café's giant pillars, and staff members meander the floor spraying off shots of air freshener, you can *still* smell the years of this historic

(and sadly dilapidated) *confitería* (café). Forget the food, the real reason to come is for the daily tango lessons and weekly *milongas* upstairs.
☎ 4601-8234; ✉ Suipacha 384, Microcentro $ US$1-5 ☾ 8am-midnight ⊙ Line B, Carlos Pellegrini; Line C, Diagonal Norte; Line D 9 de Julio

El Beso (4, A2)
This traditional salon brings in some 2000 people every week for its good, fun *milongas* and daily classes. The space upstairs has a good feel, and there's a convenient bar as you enter.
☎ 4953-2794 ✉ Riobamba 416, Microcentro $ US$2.50-3.50 ☾ from 9pm Tue, 10:30pm Wed, 6pm Thu, 11pm Sat & 10pm Sun ⊙ Line B, Callao

La Catedral (3, C2)
If tango can be casual, trendy and hip, this is where you'll find it. The rough 'n' tumble warehouse space almost adds an element of danger, especially when the trapeze artists start swinging for the Friday show. A hazy air and funky art on the walls make this more of a party, and there

are plenty of wallflowers. The best *milonga* is Tuesday.
☎ 15-5325-1630 ✉ Sarmiento 4006, Almagro ☾ classes 8:30pm Mon-Sat, *milongas* follow ⊙ Line B, Medrano

Niño Bien
Some consider Niño Bien the best *milonga* in town, which is why it's worth taking a taxi out to the Central Regional Leonesa where it's held. It boasts a great atmosphere, large ballroom and good dance floor, and gets extremely crowded, mostly with the aficionados who show up on a weekly basis.
☎ 4147-8687 ✉ Humberto 1° 1462, Constitución $ US$1-3 ☾ 9pm Thu ⊙ Line E, San Jose

Salon Canning (7, B5)
With a great dance floor, central location, traditional atmosphere and lessons for beginners prior to the *milongas*, Salon Canning makes for a wonderful evening of tango, even for novices. Well-known tango company Parakultural (www .parakultural.com.ar in Spanish) often stages lively

Centro Cultural Torquato Tasso – waving the tango flag

events involving live music, tango DJs, singers and dancers. Call for times.
☎ 4832-6753 ✉ Scalabrini Ortiz 1331, Palermo Viejo
$ US$2-3 ☽ daily 🚌 15, 57, 110, 141, 160

GAY & LESBIAN BUENOS AIRES

Angel's
Hot, humid and claustrophobic, Angel's is packed with flirtatious young men, gorgeously decked out transvestites and a smattering of straight folks who come for the fun. House music keeps the upstairs bouncing, but it's the salsa and *tropical* music downstairs that really get 'em going. It has an infectiously edgy feel.
✉ Viamonte 2168, Once
$ US$6, includes 4 drinks
☽ from 1am Thu-Sat
Ⓜ Line D, Facultad de Medicina

Bach Bar (7, C6)
This place started out as a popular lesbian club, but now brings in a mixed crowd. The live drag shows on weekends are downright raucous and keep spirits high.
✉ Cabrera 4390, Palermo
$ US$1 ☽ 10pm-late Tue-Sun 🚌 26, 106, 109, 140, 168 ♿ fair

Bulnes Class (7, D6)
A spacious, modern bar attracting a mixed but mostly gay crowd for its minimalist, chilled-out atmosphere and the fact it's easy to get a drink even when packed – the bar's smack in the middle of the room. Thursday's 'after office' means partying starts at 6pm.

GAY BA
Buenos Aires is queerer than just its nightlife. Start your night off with dinner at **Chueca** (p52), gay-friendly **Empire Thai** (p47) or **Lelé de Troya** (p54), or the outrageously fun and totally sexy **Te Mataré Ramirez** (p55). **Lugar Gay** (p73) and **Bayres B&B** (p72) are both B&Bs for men, and **Che Lulu** (p73) is an excellent low-budget, gay-friendly guesthouse.

☎ 4861-7492 ✉ Bulnes 1250, Palermo ☽ 6pm-2am Thu, 11pm-4am Fri & Sat
🚌 26, 36, 92, 106, 128
♿ good when not crowded

Contramano (2, B3)
Still packing them in after 20 years, this Recoleta landmark was one of BA's first gay clubs and still keeps the men rolling in. It attracts a mostly post-40 crowd (women aren't allowed in), and it's heavy on the pickup vibe. Male strippers take to the stage on Sunday nights. Great spot.
✉ Rodríguez Peña 1082, Recoleta $ US$3 ☽ from midnight Wed-Sun Ⓜ Line D, Callao

Glam (7, E6)
Housed on three floors inside an old mansion, this maze-like and mostly gay club is one of BA's best. No drag shows, just lots of dancing boys, casual lounge areas, stylish bars and free condoms at the door. Thursdays and Saturdays are the biggest nights.
☎ 4963-2521 ✉ Cabrera 3046, Barrio Norte $ US$5
☽ from 1am Thu-Sat
🚌 29, 92, 106, 128, 140

Pride Café (5, C1)
This comfy little café serves up 'queer coffee' (as the card proclaims) to a mostly

male clientele. A menu of sandwiches and baked goods is available. Thursday night shows range from comedy to cello and song.
☎ 4300-6435 ✉ Balcarce 869, San Telmo ☽ 10am-10pm Sun-Fri, until late Thu, closed Sat 🚌 10, 20, 45, 74, 86 ♿ fair

Sitges (7, C6)
Packed shoulder-to-shoulder on Saturday nights, this gay and lesbian 'pre-disco' plays loud, beat-laden music for an amorous crowd. On Wednesday and Thursday there's a drag show, and on Sunday there's karaoke. Come early on weekends for the aphrodisiac sushi dinner.
☎ 4861-3763 🖥 www .sitgesonline.com.ar
✉ Av Córdoba 4119, Palermo $ US$2, includes drink ☽ 10:30pm-late Wed-Sun 🚌 26, 106, 109, 140, 168 ♿ fair, front room only

UNNA (6, D3)
BA's only lesbian disco is exclusively female (sorry boys), and the womblike basement is packed with dancers, smoochers and sexy dark corners. Music ranges from pop and electronica to *salsa* and *cumbia*.
✉ Suipacha 927, Retiro
☽ from 1am Sat Ⓜ Line C, San Martín

WATCHING SPORTS
Soccer
Seeing a live soccer match is undeniably a BA highlight (see p9). Unless you're extremely savvy in potentially ugly crowd situations, sit in the pricier *platea* section where the views are also better. The *popular* area is chaos; it's where the *barra brava* (Argentina's soccer hooligans) sit.

Tickets range from US$4 to US$15 and are available at stadiums and sometimes through Ticketek (p57). The easiest way to see a game is with a guide; Tangol (p37) charges from US$35 for this privilege. Leave valuables at home and don't bring anything that might be used as a weapon. The following are BA proper's three biggest soccer clubs:

Boca Juniors (Estadio Alberto J Armando/La Bombonera; 5, D5; ☎ 4362-2260; www.boca juniors.com.ar in Spanish; Brandsen 805)

River Plate (Estadio Monumental; ☎ 4788-1200; www.cariverplate.com.ar in Spanish; Av Presidente Figueroa Alcorta 7597)

San Lorenzo (Estadio El Nuevo Gasómetro; ☎ 4918-8192; www.sanlorenzo.com.ar in Spanish; Varela 2680)

Pato
Argentina's national game, *pato* (duck), is also its strangest. Two teams of four men on horseback try to throw a leather ball with handles through a hoop at either end of a field. Gauchos invented it centuries ago playing with a dead duck wrapped in a leather sack. It was outlawed in the 19th century as, along with the ducks, players often wound up dead. Since revived, with the duck replaced by the ball, tournaments are usually held in October or November. Contact **Federación Argentina de Pato** (4, G5; ☎ 4331-0222; www.fedpato.com.ar in Spanish; 5th fl, Av Belgrano 530).

Horseracing
A day at historic **Hipódromo Argentino** (7, C1; ☎ 4778-2800; www.palermo .com.ar in Spanish; cnr Avs del Libertador & Dorrego; admission US$1-3) is a day well spent. Races are usually on Mondays and weekends. The most important is the Gran Premio Nacional in November, followed by the big December race at the famous grass track at **Hipódromo San Isidro** (☎ 4743-4010; www.hipodromosanisidro.com.ar in Spanish; Av Márquez 504) in northern Buenos Aires. San Isidro is the only grass track in the country.

Polo
Argentina is famous for polo. The season runs September to mid-November, culminating in the annual Campeonato Argentino Abierto (Argentine Open) at Palermo's **Campo Argentino de Polo** (7, B1; cnr Avs del Libertador & Dorrego). For information, contact the **Asociación Argentina de Polo** (4, F4; ☎ 5411-4777; www.aapolo.com in Spanish; Hipólito Yrigoyen 636).

THE CHOCOLATE BOX
The pride of La Boca is Boca Juniors Estadio Alberto J Armando, one of the world's most famous stadiums, popularly known as La Bombonera (The Chocolate Box). Inaugurated in 1940, the stadium sits smack in the middle of La Boca neighborhood, a spatial challenge forcing architect Luis Delpini to design it with steep seating that rises above the pitch like the walls of a box. Seeing a match here is a sporting experience second to none.

Sleeping

When it comes to big-city bang for your buck, Buenos Aires' hotels are excellent value in all but the deluxe category. When it comes to the latter, you definitely get what you pay for, but prices are similar to luxury hotels in major cities throughout the world.

The real value lies in BA's top-end and midrange boutique hotels, where you'll find warm, personal service, artsy and old-fashioned decor, and homelike comfort. Budget accommodations are also an outstanding value, especially if you don't mind (or, rather, if you prefer) smaller, more laid-back and often more eclectic abodes. The cheapest rooms at many budget hotels have shared bathrooms, but they're usually kept spotless at the hotels listed here.

All hotels serve breakfast, which is included in their rates. At deluxe and top-end hotels this usually means a continental buffet with coffee, tea and juice. Budget and midrange hotels often serve *medialunas* (croissants) with *dulce de leche* (milk caramel) or homemade jam, and coffee or tea. Boutique hotels generally provide exceptional service, though you usually won't find perks like bathrobes, room service and business centers. For that you need to go top-end or deluxe. All accommodations listed in the midrange, top-end and deluxe categories have en-suite air conditioning, a blessing during BA's hot and humid summers. Budget accommodations are generally only fan cooled.

The hotels listed here all accept reservations from abroad, requiring advance payment with a well-known credit card. They're all reputable and have given no reason to worry about fraud. The best rates for deluxe hotels are usually found by booking online.

Rates are highest and rooms fill fastest during the high season months of July and August and November through January. Always book your room with plenty of anticipation during these times or during national holidays (see p86).

ROOM RATES

Categories indicate mid- to high-season rates for a standard double room per night. Deluxe and top-end hotels tack an additional 21% tax onto their quoted prices, though this has been calculated into the following ranges.

Deluxe	US$150-300
Top End	US$75-150
Midrange	US$25-75
Budget	under $25

Service with a bow tie, Alvear Palace Hotel (p70)

DELUXE

Alvear Palace Hotel (2, C1)
By far the classiest hotel in town, the Alvear's old-world sophistication and superior service will erase the trials of that long, 1st-class flight. Bathtub Jacuzzis, Hermès toiletries, Egyptian cotton sheets, three restaurants, an elegant tea room and an indoor pool all swoop you into dreamland.
☎ 4808-2100 🖳 www .alvearpalace.com
✉ Av Alvear 1891, Recoleta
🚌 21, 45, 54, 126, 129
♿ excellent 🍴 ✕ 👶

Crowne Plaza Panamericano (4, E2)
The rooms and services are up to five-star snuff, but what this place is really about is the 23rd-floor pool and the Tomo I restaurant, one of BA's best. The pool atrium has a small bar, and the views down Av 9 de Julio are awesome.
☎ 4348-5000 ✉ Carlos Pellegrini 551, Microcentro
🚇 Line B, Carlos Pellegrini; Line C, Lavalle; Line D, 9 de Julio ♿ excellent
✕ Tomo I 🍴 👶

Faena Hotel & Universe
With Turkish baths, a spa, a beauty salon, a cabaret lounge, a business center, restaurants, a breathtaking pool and a gourmet market, 'Universe' is definitely the operative word. French designer Philippe Starke's giant five-star boutique hotel, occupying a former silo building, is the most talked about sleepery in the city.
☎ 4021-5555 🖳 www .faenaexperience.com
✉ Martha Salotti 445, Puerto Madero Este 🚌 20, 64, 93, 129, 152 & others
♿ excellent 🍴 ✕ 👶

Hotel Bel Air (6, B2)
Just off Plaza Vicente López y Planes, the Bel Air is a real gem. The lobby wine-bar and café have curving wood dividers, dark walls and mood lighting, creating an irresistible loungelike ambiance. Rooms have polished hardwood floors that beautifully complement the modern yet functional furniture reminiscent of 1960s Danish design.
☎ 4021-4000 🖳 www .hotelbelair.com.ar in Spanish ✉ Arenales 1462, Retiro 🚌 10, 21, 39, 152 & others ♿ good, one room only ✕ 👶

Loi Suites (2, C2)
Twelve floors of spacious, business-class rooms tower over the Recoleta cemetery, and those from the 9th floor up offer fabulous views of the necropolis (great if you don't mind a view of the future!). Done up in black-and-white or beige-and-white, the rooms make for a seriously plush sleep. There's a covered outdoor patio with pool too.
☎ 5777-8950 🖳 www .loisuites.com.ar ✉ Vicente López 1955, Recoleta 🚌 10, 21, 59, 60, 124 & others
♿ good, one room only
🍴 ✕ 👶

Sofitel Buenos Aires (6, D1)
Occupying the historic Torre Bencich (built in 1929, it was the city's first skyscraper), this converted art-deco landmark is regarded as one of the city's prize hotels since it opened in 2000. From the sharply designed rooms, to the library, to the jockey-club style of the café, it's pure luxury.
☎ 4131-0123/0000
🖳 www.sofitel.com
✉ Arroyo 841/849, Retiro
♿ excellent 🚇 Line C, San Martín 🍴 ✕ 👶

TOP END

Americas Towers (6, C2)
On the same block as its older sister hotel, the new Americas Towers offers comfy business digs while sticking well below the US$150 mark. Carpets in the rooms could use a spiff-up, but dark-wood headboards and armoires, and maroon curtains give the rooms a homey feel.
☎ 4815-9466 🖳 www .grupoamericas.com.ar
✉ Libertad 1070, Retiro
🚌 10, 21, 39, 132, 152 & others ♿ fair ✕ 👶

ONLY IN BUENOS AIRES
For something unique, something cool, something that screams 'This is Buenos Aires!' stay at one of the following hotels:
- Art Hotel (opposite)
- Boquitas Pintadas (p72)
- Design Suites (opposite)
- Malabia House (opposite)
- Mansión Dandi Royal (p73)

Art Hotel (2, A2)

Of BA's many new designer boutique hotels, this is the most aesthetically successful. Rooms are small, but the combination of classical and modern (the building dates from 1927) means comfort meets style head-to-head. Add a rooftop terrace and Jacuzzi and you can't go wrong.

☎ 4821-4744 🖳 www.art hotel.com.ar ✉ Azcuénaga 1268, Recoleta Ⓓ Line D, Pueyrredón

Art Suites (2, B2)

Built in 2001, Art Suites offers ultramodern yet totally comfortable apartment-style accommodations in two- or four-room units, complete with daily room service and breakfast. The four-roomers are great for families (put the kids in the *other* room!), and all are stylishly decorated.

☎ 4821-6800 🖳 www.art suites.com.ar ✉ Azcuénaga 1465, Recoleta 🚌 41, 62, 95, 101, 118 ♿

Bo Bo (7, C4)

Palermo's swankiest digs mean minimalist decor plus modern comfort, with seven rooms designed as their names suggest: Art Deco, Pop, Tecno… The two best (thanks primarily to their decks) are Minimalista and Argentina. The latter boasts a giant Jacuzzi complete with candles and skylight windows, perfect for nighttime romance. 'Rationalista' is totally wheelchair accessible.

☎ 4774-0505 🖳 www .bobohotel.com ✉ Guatemala 4882, Palermo Viejo 🚌 34, 36, 55, 93, 161 ♿ good ✕ Bo Bo ♿

Broadway All Suites (4, D2)

Smack in the theater district, Broadway All Suites offers huge rooms (even the standards have two rooms) in a generic but pleasing minimalist style, complete with acrylic green tables, couches, leather chairs and vinyl-and-wood headboards. A current expansion will up the room count from 66 to 108.

☎ 4378-9300 🖳 www .broadway-suites.com.ar ✉ Av Corrientes 1173, Congreso Ⓑ Line B, Carlos Pellegrine; Line D, Tribunales ♿ fair ♿

Dazzler Hotel (6, C3)

Considering the comfortable rooms, the giant lobby and the prime location near Plaza Libertad, the Dazzler is excellent value. Vinyl-and-wood headboards and drab mustard decor (even the marble bathroom floors have a yellowish hue) give it a slightly passé feel, but it's spotless and inviting nonetheless.

☎ 4816-5005 🖳 www .dazzlerhotel.com ✉ Libertad 902, Retiro Ⓓ 5, 10, 21, 67, 152 & others ✕ ♿

Design Suites (2, C3)

From the single-lane pool in the cement-floor lobby to the en-suite espresso makers, it's top-to-bottom fun here for the minimalist in everyone. Tables, chairs, paintings, glasses – everything was designed specifically for Design Suites, meaning you'll never find a place quite like it.

☎ 4814-8700 🖳 www .designsuites.com ✉ MT de Alvear 1683, Recoleta Ⓓ Line D, Callao ♿ ✕ ♿

Art Hotel's artful entrance

Malabia House (7, B5)

This beautifully renovated house has 15 luxurious bedrooms, stocked with modern furnishings, terry-cloth robes and slippers. Common spaces are gracious and include tiny courtyard gardens. Candles, soft music and a comfortable homey feel add peace and romance, while the service is excellent. Plus, it's Palermo!

☎ 4832-3345 🖳 www .malabiahouse.com.ar ✉ Malabia 1555, Palermo 🚌 15, 57, 110, 141, 160 ♿ difficult ♿

NH City Hotel (4, G4)

While adhering strictly to BA minimalism, NH City's rooms are supremely comfortable, thanks to the deep-umber and earth-tone walls, plush chairs, fabric headboards, and mustard-and-maroon curtains or bedspreads. The rooftop pool and the gourmet buffet breakfast cinch the knot.

☎ 4121-6464 🖳 www .nh-hotels.com ✉ Bolívar 160, Microcentro Ⓔ Line E, Bolívar ♿ excellent ✕ ♿

MIDRANGE

Ayacucho Palace Hotel
(2, B2)
The 64 clean and modern wood-floored rooms here are comfortable yet non-descript. It's a fair deal for the Recoleta area, and you're only a bone's throw away from the famous cemetery and weekend craft fair.
☎ 4806-1815 ☐ www .ayacuchohotel.com.ar ✉ Ayacucho 1408, Recoleta 🚌 10, 21, 59, 60, 110 & others ✕ ♿

Bayres B&B (3, C2)
Formerly the owner's home, this fabulously decorated gay B&B offers classy comfort in Palermo. Perks include free Internet and staff who can point you to the best bars in town.
☎ 4772-3877 ☐ www .bayresbnb.com ✉ Av Córdoba 5842, Palermo 🚌 21, 39, 93, 151, 168

Boquitas Pintadas
Likely the most bizarre guesthouse you'll visit, this German-owned and self-proclaimed 'pop hotel' offers eccentric rooms in a converted early-1900s house. The giant rooms have a mix of '50s pop and classically styled furnishings and changing en-suite art exhibits such as garbage-bag macramé. DJs spin on weekend nights in the restaurant-bar.
☎ 4381-6064, 4382-4096 ☐ www.boquitas -pintadas.com.ar ✉ Estados Unidos 1399, Monserrat 🚌 39, 53, 60, 96, 126 & others ✕

WHERE TO LAY YOUR HEAD
Sleeping in pricey **Recoleta** is great, thanks to its location between Palermo and downtown, and the proximity of the cemetery, parks and plazas. Deluxe hotels are mostly in **Puerto Madero** and the **Microcentro**. The former is urban La La Land with little action outside the hotel, but its proximity to San Telmo and the Microcentro is a plus. The latter means urban madness the minute you step outside into the heart of BA. **Palermo** is unbeatable for nightlife, eating and shopping and a lovely area to wake up to. **San Telmo** is touristy and dark at night, but delightfully old-fashioned and close to the Microcentro.

Casa Monserrat
An intricate facade hides what's likely the most stunning B&B in BA. Casa Monserrat occupies a restored 1870 home, with a garden, overhanging roofs, handsome iron columns, high ceilings and beautifully carved doors. Rooms are stylish, well lit and divinely comfortable. The only drawback is the slightly seedy neighborhood.
☎ 4304-8798 ☐ www .casa-monserrat.com ✉ Salta 1074, Monserrat ⊕ Line E, San José ♿ fair, narrow doorways ♿

Castelar Hotel & Spa
(4, D4)
Little has changed since the doors opened in 1929: service is tops, rooms are spiffy and the downstairs *confitería* (café) remains a BA classic. It's worth forking out extra for the bigger, more luxurious 'superior' rooms. The spa (see p85) is a step back in time.
☎ 4383-5000 ☐ www .castelarhotel.com.ar ✉ Av de Mayo 1152, Microcentro ⊕ Line A, Lima ✕ Confitería Castelar ♿ limited ♿

Hotel Facón Grande
(4, G1)
Bringing a touch of country life to the city, Facón Grande (Big Dagger) offers plain but comfortable rooms atop an airy lobby bedecked with traditional Argentine textiles and ceramic vessels. The ascot- and cap-wearing staff follow suit. There's a kids' playroom too.
☎ 4312-6360 ☐ www .hotelfacongrande.com in Spanish ✉ Reconquista 645, Microcentro ⊕ Line B, LN Alem ♿

Hotel Frossard (4, F1)
Two blocks from the theater strip, this little gem in big Microcentro was originally owned by relatives of Che Guevarra. It's a simple, beautifully restored, nine-room B&B, with high ceilings and loads of ornate trim work. For the price, it's superb.
☎ 4322-1811 ☐ www .hotelfrossard.com ✉ Tucumán 686, Microcentro ⊕ Line B, Florida; Line C, Lavalle ♿

Hotel Principado (6, E3)
It ain't the Ritz, but it's comfortable nonetheless, and

its enviable location between pedestrianized Florida and the beautiful Plaza San Martín make Principado a solid choice. Wrought-iron, ranch-style chandeliers bedeck the understated lobby. Rooms are drab but totally fine.
☎ 4313-3022 🖳 www.principado.com.ar ✉ Paraguay 481, Retiro 🚇 20, 22, 62, 129, 152 & others ♿ limited ✕ ♨

Lugar Gay (5, C2)
Unsigned and conveniently situated near Plaza Dorrego, BA's first gay B&B occupies a handsomely converted house with small, pleasant rooms, a Jacuzzi, and a three-level rooftop terrace where the boys (it's all male) bronze their bodies in the afternoon sun.
☎ 4300-4747 🖳 www.lugargay.org ✉ Defensa 1120, San Telmo 🚍 9, 10, 29, 45, 126 & others

Mansión Dandi Royal (5, B1)
Eat, sleep, drink and dance tango by shacking up here, BA's self-proclaimed 'tango residential academy' where everything – from the paintings, decorations, onsite classes and, of course, music – is tango. Occupying a spectacular early-1900s San Telmo mansion, it boasts king-sized

Freshen up with Frida at Che Lulu

beds, claw-foot tubs, a rooftop lap pool, a basement gym and, of course, a dance studio.
☎ 4361-3537 🖳 www.mansiondandiroyal.com ✉ Piedras 922/936, San Telmo 🚍 17, 20, 59, 67, 195 & others 🚭 ✕

BUDGET

Che Lulu (7, B4)
With a different local designer decorating each room, it's no wonder Che Lulu is a hit. Style, co-owner Rodrigo's charisma and the prime location make for a winning combo in the budget category. Rooms are miniature, and some lack windows, but the beautifully designed common area more than makes up for it. The cheapest sleeps are in the upstairs dorm room.
☎ 4772-0289 🖳 www.luluguesthouse.com ✉ Emilio Zolá 5185, Palermo Viejo 🚍 21, 11, 161, 166 ♨

Como en Casa (7, C4)
One of the first digs in Palermo Viejo, Como en Casa's selling points are its cozy, rustically decorated common area (complete with colonial-style accoutrements and decorative crafts), its supreme location and its friendly, knowledgeable staff. Rooms are a bit basic, and some have shared bathrooms, but you won't spend much time inside them, will you?
☎ 4831-0517 🖳 www.bandb.com.ar ✉ Gurruchaga 2155, Palermo Viejo 🚍 34, 36, 55, 93 ♨

El Sol de San Telmo (5, B2)
With an onsite dance floor, communal kitchen and 12

unique rooms, this cozy guesthouse occupies a converted 1890 house and offers guests an easy entrance into BA tango. Tango aside, it's a delightful place to stay, considering the giant rooftop terrace, friendly owners, and old-fashioned rooms. The cheapest rooms have shared bathrooms.
☎ 4300-4394 🖳 www.elsoldesantelmo.com ✉ Chacabuco 1181, San Telmo 🚇 Line C, San Juan ♨

Gran Hotel Hispano (4, E4)
Don't let the cavernous lobby put you off: above it, three floors of old-fashioned rooms open onto a narrow, sun-filled patio making for one of BA's best budget hotels. There's a plant-filled sundeck to boot. Beds are a little rickety and the flower decor can be overwhelming, but it's still a winner. There are plenty of eating options nearby.
☎ 4345-2020 🖳 www.hhispano.com.ar ✉ Av de Mayo 861, Microcentro 🚇 Line A, Piedras; Line C, Av de Mayo ♨

La Otra Orilla (7, C5)
In 2003, mother and daughter duo Cecilia and Agustina opened their converted 1937 home to accommodate travelers, offering a lovely place to lay the weary head. Rooms are delightfully furnished with old armoires and such, and the living room and outdoor patio make you feel right at home.
☎ 4867-4070 🖳 www.otraorilla.com.ar ✉ Julián Alvarez 1779, Palermo 🚍 36, 160, 188 ♨

About Buenos Aires

HISTORY

Buenos Aires, like Argentina, has a tumultuous history, rocked between brutal dictatorships, periods of unprecedented wealth and decades of military rule.

Backwater Port Turns Capital

Buenos Aires was founded twice. The first in 1536, under leadership of Spaniard Pedro de Mendoza, failed after settlers were ousted by the indigenous Querandí, who had populated the banks of the Río de la Plata for tens of thousands of years. Juan de Garay reestablished Buenos Aires in 1580, planting the Spanish flag somewhere around Parque Lezama.

The town remained a backwater, however, since the Spanish Crown focused its empire building on the silver-rich territory of Alto Perú and restricted trade through the peripheral port of Buenos Aires. So Buenos Aires' merchants turned to contraband. By 1776, the increas-

By 1776, Buenos Aires had lionized its position as an important trading port

ing wealth passing through the port finally forced Spain to make Buenos Aires the capital of the new Viceroyalty of the Río de la Plata.

Independence & the Golden Age

The British were also amassing an empire, and decided to claim the port in 1806 and 1807. The local porteños (as the port's inhabitants were called) beat them back to their ships, pouring cauldrons of boiling oil and water from the rooftops and firing cannons from balconies. The successful expulsion of British troops gave criollos (Argentine-born colonists) new confidence to stand apart from Spain, and they declared independence on May 25, 1810. Formal independence was declared on July 9, 1816, in the city of Tucumán.

EVITA, LADY OF HOPE

From her humble origins in the Pampas to her rise to power beside President Juan Perón, Eva María Duarte de Perón is one of the most revered political figures on the planet. Known affectionately as Evita, she is Argentina's beloved First Lady, in some ways even eclipsing the legacy of her husband. Although many argue the Peróns ruled by decree rather than consent, while her husband was in office Evita reached out to the poor and elderly. In 1947 she helped give women the vote. When she died of cancer at age 33, Evita probably had no idea she'd later enjoy near-saint status and be a pop icon after the release of *Evita* (starring Madonna, a serious bone of contention in Argentina).

After a lengthy civil war, a succession of presidents and the creation of Argentina's constitution, the country finally moved into a golden age of prosperity which lasted from the late 1800s until 1929. During this time, many of the fine buildings that characterize Buenos Aires today were built. European immigrants flooded in, increasing the city's population seven fold between 1869 and 1895. Industry was unable to absorb mass immigration, and labor unrest grew. With the onset of the Great Depression, the military took power under conditions of considerable social unease. An obscure colonel, Juan Domingo Perón, was the first leader to try to come to grips with Argentina's economic crisis.

Perón to Alfonsín

With the help of his charismatic wife, Eva (Evita) Perón, Juan Perón became president in 1946. Although they ruled by decree rather than consent, the Peróns championed working-class causes. But economic difficulties and Evita's death in 1952 undermined Perón's second presidency. In late 1955, a military coup sent him into exile in Spain and initiated nearly three decades of catastrophic military rule.

Perón returned to Argentina in 1973, became president again, and died a year later. On March 24, 1976, a bloodless military coup took control of the Argentine government and began the period known as the Dirty War. Between 1976 and 1983, human rights groups estimate that some 30,000 people were killed or 'disappeared.'

From national icon to pop-culture icon: Argentina's beloved Evita

By 1982, military rule began losing any legitimacy. In an attempt to drum up support for the government, the regime launched an invasion to dislodge the British from the Falkland Islands, which Argentina claimed as its own. Underestimating a severe British response, Argentina surrendered after only 74 days, with the military regime left in tatters. Civilian Raúl Alfonsín was elected president in 1983.

Buenos Aires Today

Carlos Ménem succeeded Alfonsín, and ushered in a period of false economic stability (largely a result of pegging the peso to the US dollar) and rampant government corruption. The latter finally forced his resignation in 1999. With the peso pegged to the dollar, Argentina was unable to compete on the international market. State coffers were empty, and by 2001, the economy teetered on collapse. Amid nationwide protests (the biggest of which were in BA) over a government freeze on bank withdrawals, Ménem's successor, Fernando de la Rúa (formerly BA's mayor), resigned. Three interim presidents also resigned by the time Eduardo Duhalde took office in January 2002. Duhalde devalued the peso that month and announced Argentina would default on US$140 billion in foreign debt. Since then, with the peso hovering around three to the dollar, things have settled down, and there's even a sense of optimism with current president Nestor Kirchner.

ENVIRONMENT

Buenos Aires sits at the mouth of the Río de la Plata, on the eastern edge of the vast Argentine grasslands known as the Pampas. As one of the world's megacities, Buenos Aires suffers typical environmental problems that result from over-population. Both noise (honking cars and roaring buses) and air pollution are factors of everyday life. Fortunately, frequent rains clear the air of smog. City streets are generally clean, except in residential neighborhoods where dog feces and urine can make for a slippery, smelly walk.

Bustling Microcentro, Buenos Aires' chaotic center

Buenos Aires' waterways – most visibly the Riachuelo in the barrio of La Boca – are cesspools of industrial contamination. Despite Argentina's self-sufficiency in petroleum and hydroelectric capacity, the government has promoted nuclear power since 1950. The capital lacks an official recycling system, though a huge number of people, known as *cartoneros,* make their living picking over the city for anything they can sell to recycling centers.

GOVERNMENT & POLITICS

Buenos Aires is the capital of Argentina and officially known as the Ciudad Autónoma de Buenos Aires. The title denotes its standing as an independent district, similar to Washington, DC. It lies within the province of Buenos Aires, but the provincial capital is at La Plata, 60km east.

Traditionally, Argentina's president appointed the mayor of Buenos Aires, but constitutional reform in 1996 permitted Fernando de la Rúa to become the BA's first elected mayor. The current mayor is Aníbal Ibarra. Politics can be a touchy subject; to the visitor, it most visibly manifests itself in the almost daily protests around Plaza de Mayo. These protests are generally peaceful and are usually carried out by groups of *piqueteros* (picketers) who block city streets to demand basic social services or commemorate political events. President Nestor Kirchner recently threatened to crack down on these protests, which many porteños feel occur with unfair frequency.

ECONOMY

When 'convertability' (the pegging of the peso to the US dollar) was scrapped and the government announced it would convert bank accounts at a rate of 1.4 pesos per dollar, everyone with money still in Argentine banks lost over half their dollar value. For Argentines holding US dollars, it was a landslide, and many bought second homes in the provinces or more property in the capital. For most, however, it was disaster. Argentina's sizable middle class was left in shambles, and 52% of the population now live below the poverty line. In 2005 unemployment hovered at around 18%.

> **DID YOU KNOW?**
> • The average monthly rent for a furnished two-bedroom apartment in Palermo Viejo is US$550; for locals with a *garantía* (cosignatory) the same goes for about US$250.
> • Buenos Aires' most expensive real estate is in Recoleta, Palermo Chico and Puerto Madero.
> • Buenos Aires has the highest number of psychoanalysts per capita in the world.
> • Buenos Aires sees about seven million tourists every year.

There may be signs of light. President Kirchner negotiated a massive debt swap, reducing the amount Argentina must pay to foreign bond holders. Exports have skyrocketed and local industry has bounced back. Arriving in Buenos Aires as a foreigner, you'd hardly know the economic mayhem the country just went through.

SOCIETY & CULTURE

Between 1870 and 1920, over six million people immigrated to Argentina, the majority of whom stayed in Buenos Aires. People came from Eastern Europe, Britain, Portugal, France and other European countries, but the vast majority came from Italy and Spain. Buenos Aires' new arrivals gave the city pizza, tango, *lunfardo* (Buenos Aires slang), *filete* (p22), soccer and – most visibly – its expressive and oh-so-Italian way of talking.

Buenos Aires also has one of the world's largest Jewish populations, most of whom live in the barrio of Once or the northern neighborhood of Belgrano. Within the city there are small Japanese and Middle Eastern communities. More recent immigrants have come from Asian countries like Korea, Taiwan and China. The neighborhood of Belgrano has its own little China Town.

All that said, the city still has the predominant flavor of Europe – not quite the melting pot of New York or London. Roman Catholicism remains the officially supported religion of Argentina, and while most porteños don't attend mass, many cross themselves when passing churches or dangle rosaries from their rearview mirrors.

Every man and his dog is attracted to the greens of Palermo

Etiquette

Despite its enormity, Buenos Aires is a remarkably friendly city. Stopping someone on the street to ask directions is completely normal, and more often than not leads to friendly conversation about your origin and why you're in BA. Many porteños speak some English and love the chance to practice it on a native speaker. Although Buenos Aires is known for its fashionable residents, it's also surprisingly casual: jeans are acceptable at most restaurants and clubs, and shorts and tennis shoes are fine for beating around town in summer. During introductions, women always exchange a kiss on the cheek, and men shake hands. Among friends, men also exchange the cheek kiss. Pleasantries are the best intro to any conversation, and no exchange begins without a polite *'buenos días'* (good morning) or *'buenas tardes'* (good afternoon).

ARTS
Architecture

As Spain built its South American colonial empire, it focused its energy on silver-rich Alto Perú and parts of northern Argentina. Colonial architecture is therefore minimal compared to other Latin American cities. Most of the surviving structures are found in San Telmo and Monserrat. Where Buenos Aires really shines architecturally is in its mid-19th- and early-20th-century buildings, all constructed during Argentina's golden era. Between 1880 and 1890 the city was literally rebuilt and many of its grandest buildings, plazas and parks date to this time. Italianate styles characterized much of the early building, but toward the end of the 19th century, French influences crept in to give the city its Parisian flair. Art-nouveau architecture, of which there are many showpieces standing today, hit the city in the early 1900s and art-deco constructions followed in the 1930s. Contemporary architecture is mainly focused around Puerto Madero, which was only recently opened to development.

Golden-era architecture

Literature

Buenos Aires is a literary city, with the bookstores, newsstands, book fairs and authors to prove it. One of the 20th century's greatest writers, Jorge Luis Borges (1899–1986) penned fiction, nonfiction and poetry, much of which is set outside his former home of Buenos Aires. His stories are amassed into the tome *Collected Fictions*, which is translated into English. The other 20th-century great is Julio Cortázar (1914–84), whose most famous book, *Hopscotch* (which can be read in two different directions) is a milestone in modern fiction. Another of the Borges generation is Ernesto Sábato (1911–), whose complex and uncompromising novels have been extremely influential on later Argentine literature. Other influential porteño writers include Adolfo Bioy Casares and sisters Silvina and Victoria Ocampo.

Less known to outsiders, José Hernández wasn't a porteño but he did write one of the country's most important books, *Martín Fierro* (1872), an epic poem about gaucho life. It's sold in a variety of formats and languages throughout Buenos Aires and makes a great piece of literature to take home.

Music

Tango (p10 and p65) is a porteño thing. Argentina's folk music is known as *folklórica*. Styles such as *chamamé, chacarera, samba,* and the *carnavlito* are all beautiful mixes of traditional Andean music and old European rhythms. Buenos Aires' many *peñas* (folk venues) are where you go to hear this infectious music. One of the

NEW SOUNDS

One of the latest crazes to sweep BA is *cumbia villera,* hardboiled gangsta-style *cumbia* music boiling up from the city's *villeras* (poor neighborhoods). It's almost strictly working class, unlike the other new sound of *tango electrónica.* The best-known in this genre is Bajofondo Tango Club.

nation's greatest *folklórica* singers was Altahuapa Yupanqui. Modern folk musicians include the astounding Mercedes Sosa and Los Chalchaleros.

Argentina also has a rich rock-and-roll heritage (called *rock nacional*), and musicians like Fito Páez and Charlie García are national icons. Soda Stereo and Grammy winners Los Fabulosos Cadillacs are both excellent. Contemporary rock and rollers include Bersuit Vergarabat (undeniably one of rock's greatest bands), and lesser pop greats like Babasónicos, Divididos, Patricio Rey y sus Redonditos de Ricota and Los Ratones Paranóicos. Kevin Johansen, who sings in English and Spanish, is modern Leonard Cohen–meets–Argentine folk and one of the country's best. See p61 for information on live-music venues.

A *folklórica* singer – all miked up and ready to folk

Film

Not surprisingly, Buenos Aires is the center of Argentine cinema. One of the city's most internationally renowned directors is Juan José Campanella, whose *El hijo de la novia* (Son of the Bride) received an Oscar nomination for best foreign-language film in 2002. Another big name is Fabián Bielinsky, whose *Nueve reinas* (Nine Queens; 2000) tells the twist-of-fate story of two minor Buenos Aires conmen. Luis Puenzo's *The Official Story* (1985) deals with the Dirty War and also won an Oscar for best foreign-language film. Today's cutting-edge Argentine directors include Lucrecia Martel, whose outstanding *La Ciénaga* (The Swamp; 2001) follows two families suffering through a heavy vacation in Salta province. Another award-winning director is Pablo Trapero, whose gritty *El bonaerense* (2002) explores the corruption within Buenos Aires' police culture. Carlos Solín's internationally award-winning *Historias minimas* (Minimal Stories; 2002) and his more recent *Bonbón, el perro* (Bonbón the Dog; 2004) are both outstanding.

Directory

ARRIVAL & DEPARTURE
Air
Nearly all international flights arrive at Buenos Aires' Aeropuerto Internacional Ministro Pistarini, better known as Ezeiza. Traveling the 35km from the airport to town takes about 45 minutes by cab or shuttle, and up to 1½ hours by bus. Domestic flights and flights to/from Uruguay leave from **Aeroparque Jorge Newbery** (3, C1; Av Costanera Rafael Obligado, Costanera Norte) a short distance from downtown.

INFORMATION
General inquiries & flight information (☎ 5480-6111)
Website www.aa2000.com.ar

AIRPORT ACCESS
Ezeiza
Bus Public bus No 86 makes the slow slog into town (US$0.50; up to 1½ hours). Catch it outside the Aerolíneas Argentinas terminal, a short walk from the international terminal.
Shuttle Manuel Tienda León (MTL; www.tiendaleon.com) offers fast, fairly priced shuttles to/from downtown (US$8.50) every half hour. Hotel drop-off/pickup is free within city center; if your hotel is elsewhere, take the service to/from the downtown **office** (6, E1; ☎ 4314-3636; Av Madero 1299 at San Martín). MTL's airport office sits directly outside customs.
Taxi Taxi stands are inside the airport and just outside the main entrance. All charge about US$16, including tolls. MTL's taxi service is more expensive.

Aeroparque Jorge Newbery
Bus Public bus Nos 33 and 45 head to the center; don't cross the street when you exit the airport – take them going south. MTL shuttles also run to the center (US$3).
Taxi A taxi to the center of town costs about US$4.

Bus
Buenos Aires' modern **Retiro bus terminal** (3, D2; ☎ 4310-0700; Av Ramos Mejía 1680, Retiro) has excellent bus connections throughout Argentina and to/from most South American capital cities. Hundreds of bus companies serve Retiro (not to be confused with nearby Estación Retiro train station) and are grouped together according to destination. Long-distance buses range from comfortable to luxurious, and baggage is safe in their lower holds; get a claim ticket and be sure to tip.

Retiro is walking distance from the north end of pedestrianized Florida, and a cab to anywhere in the center should cost no more than US$3.

Train
Trains serve Buenos Aires' suburbs and nearby provinces. Below are the most useful train stations (all served by Subte; p82) and their destinations.

ESTACIÓN CONSTITUCIÓN (5, A4)
Roca line (☎ 4304-0028) To the southern suburbs, Rosario, La Plata, Bahía Blanca, Atlantic beach towns.

ESTACIÓN LACROZE (3, B2)
Urquiza line (☎ 0-800-777-3377) To the northwestern suburbs.

ESTACIÓN ONCE (3, D2)
Sarmiento line (☎ 0-800-333-3822) To the southwestern suburbs, Luján, Santa Rosa.

ESTACIÓN RETIRO (6, D1)
Belgrano line (☎ 0-800-777-3377) To the northern suburbs.
Mitre line (☎ 4317-4445) To Tigre, Rosario.
San Martín (☎ 4959-0800) To the northern suburbs.

Boat
There are several river crossings between Uruguay and Buenos Aires that involve ferry or hydrofoil; some require combinations

with buses. Ferries leave from the **Buque-bus terminal** (6, F3; ☎ 4316-6500; www .buquebus.com in Spanish) at Av Antártida Argentina and Córdoba.

To/from Colonia Daily ferries (one way US$18-24, three hours) and hydrofoils (one way US$31-41, one hour), with direct bus connections to Montevideo (three hours more).

To/from Montevideo Daily high-speed ferries from BA (one way US$54-70, three hours).

To/from Piriápolis In summer, a three-hour ferry ride connects the resort town of Piriápolis with BA at least once a day.

Travel Documents

PASSPORTS
Passports must be valid for six months from date of entry.

VISAS
Nationals of Australia, USA, Canada, New Zealand and most Western European countries do not need visas to visit Argentina, but must obtain a free tourist card (good for up to 90 days) upon arrival. Flight attendants hand them out during incoming flights.

RETURN/ONWARD TICKETS
A return/onward ticket is officially required but rarely asked for.

Customs & Duty-Free
Items for personal use, including cameras, laptops and binoculars are duty-free (they cannot be new or for commercial use). Be certain to declare expensive personal items such as laptops to avoid suspicion that you will resell them. Visitors are allowed 2L of alcohol, 400 cigarettes and new goods up to a value of US$300 duty-free. If entering from neighboring countries, these amounts are reduced to 1L of alcohol, 200 cigarettes and up to only US$100 in new goods.

Departure Tax
An international departure tax is levied on flights leaving Argentina and is *rarely* included in the price of your ticket. You must pay the tax in Argentine pesos (AR$54) or US dollars (US$18) after check-in and have the tax sticker placed on your ticket.

Left Luggage
Left luggage is available at Ezeiza airport and is located next to the Farmacity store on the ground floor of level A.

GETTING AROUND
With a modern underground (the Subte), a labyrinthine 24-hour bus system and a plethora of affordable taxis, Buenos Aires is cheap and easy to get around. Relying on public transport, however, does require a bit of initial studying. The capital is a very walkable city, unless you need to get across town fast. If so, the Subte or a cab is your best bet. In this book, the nearest Subte or bus line is noted after the Ⓢ or 🚌 icon for each listing.

Bus
Buenos Aires has a huge and complex *colectivo* (bus) system, and the only way to make any sense of it is by purchasing a *Guía T* (bus guidebook). These pocketbooks are sold at most newsstands for US$1, and will become your new best friend. Locate your destination street in the street index, flip to the indicated map page and grid box, then match a bus number from that box to your departure box and you're off. Most routes (but not all) run 24 hours. Most rides cost AR$0.80 (US$0.27). When you get on, tell the driver *'ochenta'* (80) and drop the money in the machine.

Subte
BA's Subte opened in 1913 and is the quickest way to get around the city, though it's usually hot and crowded. At the close of this edition, it consisted of lines A, B, C, D

and E; a new H line was due to open up in 2006/07.

Single-ride magnetic cards cost AR$0.70 (about US$0.24) and can be purchased at *boleterías* (ticket booths) in all Subte stations. To save time, buy a five- or 10-ride card, since queues can get backed up. At some stations, the tracks separate the platforms, so make sure of your direction *before* passing through the turnstiles. Trains operate 5am to 10pm Monday to Saturday and 8am to 10pm on Sundays. Service is frequent on weekdays, slower on weekends.

Train

For getting around the city, the only train that really comes in handy is the Mitre line (running between Retiro and Tigre), which makes getting from Retiro to Las Cañitas or Belgrano's Barrio China (China Town) a snap.

Taxi & Remise

BA's ubiquitous black-and-yellow taxis ply the city day and night; you rarely have to wait longer than it takes to step to any curb and throw your arm up. Ranks are only occasionally used. Tipping is not expected, though leaving the small change is customary. The starting fair is AR$1.60 (about US$0.53), and drivers should always use the *taxímetro* (taxi meter). Most rides within the city cost US$2 to US$4. There are no tolls within the city.

Remises (radio taxis) look like regular cars and don't have meters. They cost about the same as street taxis but you're less likely to get ripped off, since a fare is always established beforehand. Most hotels and restaurants will call a *remise* for you. It's also a handy way to the airport.

Car & Motorcycle

On a short trip to Buenos Aires, getting behind the wheel is a good way to turn an enjoyable visit into a whirl through insanity. Porteños drive like maniacs, and without the time to adjust to the road, you're better off relying on public transport. However, if you do need to hire a vehicle, try **Avis**

(6, C1; ☎ 4326-5542; www.avis.com.ar; Cerrito 1527), **New Way Rent a Car** (6, D3; ☎ 4515-0331; www.new-wayrenta car.com.ar; MT de Alvear 773) or **Hertz** (6, C3; ☎ 4816-8001; www.hertz.com.ar; Paraguay 1138).

PRACTICALITIES
Business Hours

General business hours for offices are 8am to 5pm Monday to Friday. Most stores stay open until 7pm or 8pm and open 9am to 1pm or 2pm on Saturdays as well. Most banks close by 3pm and are open on Saturday 9am to 1pm. Restaurants generally open daily from noon to 4pm for lunch and from 8pm to midnight or later for dinner. Cafés are open from early morning until after 8pm and often much later. Tourist offices open from 8am or 9am to between 8pm and 10pm daily. Shopping centers generally operate from 10am to 10pm daily.

Climate & When to Go

Remember, because it's in the southern hemisphere, BA's seasons are opposite those of the northern hemisphere: summer runs November to January, fall February to April, winter May to July and spring August to October. Summers are hot and humid, and winters can drop to bone-chilling cold, especially on humid or windy days. Spring and fall are pleasantly humid. BA has an annual rainfall of 900mm.

Spring and fall – which are also tourist low seasons – are the best times to visit, though the hot summer nights make for a wonderful experience. Winters are fine, really, but make sure you bring a warm jacket.

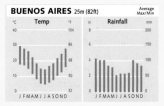

BUENOS AIRES 25m (82ft)

Disabled Travelers

Travelers with disabilities will find getting around somewhat difficult, but not impossible. Negotiating Buenos Aires' narrow, busy and uneven sidewalks in a wheelchair can be a challenge. Crossing streets can be tricky, since not every corner has ramps, and Argentine drivers have little patience. Nevertheless, Argentines with disabilities do get around, and there exist a few buses described as *piso bajo,* which lower to provide wheelchair lifts.

Throughout this book, listings marked with a ♿ icon are wheelchair accessible. Every place is different, of course, but as a general guideline we have graded the accessibility of establishments following the icon. 'Excellent' means the place is easily accessible, is easy to get around, and has accessible bathrooms (if there are any). 'Good' means the entrance is fine, and moving about inside is, for the most part, manageable. 'Fair' means you may have to negotiate a step or two to get in, and once you're inside, certain areas may be tricky. 'Limited' means you can get a wheelchair in, but it's going to be difficult.

Importantly, restaurant dining rooms are usually wheelchair accessible, but their bathrooms often are not. Bathrooms are regularly up or down a flight of stairs and/or behind a narrow doorway. Play it safe and assume the bathrooms will be inaccessible.

INFORMATION & ORGANIZATIONS

In Buenos Aires, **Movidisc** (4, E3; ☎ 4328-6921; www.movidisc-web.com.ar in Spanish; 3rd fl, Av Roque Sáenz Peña 868) offers private transportation and day tours in vans fully equipped for wheelchair users. If you're taking a tour with another agency, Movidisc can provide transportation alone, provided you ask your tour company to arrange it with Movidisc.

Online, check out:

Access-able Travel Source (www.access-able.com)

accesible.com (www.accesible.com)

Mobility International (www.miusa.org)

Discounts

STUDENT & YOUTH CARDS

The International Student Identity Card (ISIC), available for US$11 through the student and discount travel agency **Asatej** (6, E3; ☎ 4114-7500; www.asatej.net in Spanish; Room 320, 3rd fl, Galería Buenos Aires, Florida 835), can help travelers obtain discounts on museum admissions.

SENIORS' CARDS

Travelers over the age of 60 can sometimes obtain senior-citizen discounts on museum admissions and the like. Usually a passport with date of birth is sufficient evidence of age. There are no seniors' cards in BA.

Electricity

Argentina operates on 220V AC 50Hz. There are two types of electric plugs: those with two round prongs (as in Europe) and those with three angled, flat prongs (as in Australia and New Zealand); see http://kropla.com/electric2.htm for more details. To use a US laptop that doesn't have a built in 110–220V converter, you'll need a transformer *and* an adaptor. The former must be rated for electronic equipment — converters sold at most travel stores are for hairdryers or battery chargers and can fry your machine. Both are available at *ferreterías* (hardware stores) throughout the city.

Embassies

Australia (3, C1; ☎ 4779-3500; Villanueva 1400, Palermo)

Canada (☎ 4808-1000; Tagle 2828, Palermo)

France (6, D2; ☎ 4312-2409; 4th fl, Av Santa Fe 846, Retiro)

UK (2, B1; ☎ 4808-2000; Dr Luis Agote 2412, Recoleta)

USA (7, D3; ☎ 5777-4533; Colombia 4300, Palermo)

Emergencies

Despite what every Argentine *outside* BA thinks, the capital is safe for tourists. As in any big city, there are rough neighborhoods, but areas with any tourist appeal are generally fine. One exception is La Boca, which can get iffy outside the obvious tourist areas. Crimes against tourists are mostly of the pickpocketing, short-changing type – things the savvy traveler can easily guard against. Neighborhoods that draw you out at night are usually safe, with the exception of the western reaches of San Telmo, Constitución and La Boca. Stay conscious of your surroundings and avoid wandering down strange side streets with a digital SLR camera and a fat money pouch hanging off your neck. The most serious scam you're likely to run across is the 'Duh, which way do I go?' taxi driver.

In case of an emergency:
Ambulance (☎ 107)
Fire (☎ 100)
Police (☎ 101)
Rape crisis line (☎ 4981-6882; 4958-4291)
Tourist police (4, G2; ☎ 4346-5748, 0-800-999-5000; Av Corrientes 436, ⏱ 24hr)

Fitness

It's not uncommon to see someone clad in Spandex standing outside a gymnasium entrance puffing on a fag, or – and this species is a particularly fun one to spot – the smoking jogger. Porteños have a very mixed take on fitness. And smokes or not, a lot of them love it, which is why you'll have no problem finding everything from day spas and yoga classes to muscle houses and Pilates. Jogging in Palermo's parks is excellent.

DAY SPAS

For a step back in time, try the spa at Castelar Hotel & Spa (p72), built in 1929. In the steam-filled gentlemen's lounge, robed men read the newspaper while they smoke cigarettes and sip Gancia. Next door, women treat themselves to everything from hair brushings to pedicures.

Aqua Vita Spa (2, B3; ☎ 4812-5989; www.aquavitamedicalspa.com in Spanish; Arenales 1965) is a small, futuristically lit spa in Recoleta. Services include facials, sauna, hydromassage, crystal and stone massage, and exfoliation. Rates vary widely for the many services, but start at around US$40.

HEALTH CLUBS

Buenos Aires' biggest gym chain is **Megatlon** (4, G2; ☎ 4322-7884; www.megatlon.com in Spanish; Reconquista 335) with over a dozen branches throughout the city. Most have athletic courts, many have pools (including the Reconquista branch), and all have classes, weights and machines. Day passes cost about US$5.

YOGA & PILATES

Pilates hit BA big time, thanks mostly to 'Pilates Queen' Tamara Di Tella who has numerous branches of her candidly named **Tamara Di Tella Pilates** (7, E4; ☎ 4833-0603; www.cuerpodiet.com in Spanish; cnr Aráoz & Juncal; ⏱ 8am-9pm Mon-Fri, 9am-2pm Sat; four sessions US$25) throughout the city.

Vida Natural (7, F6; ☎ 4826-1695; www.yogacentro.com.ar in Spanish; Charcas 2852; ⏱ 8:30am-12:30pm & 2-8:30pm Mon-Fri, 8:30am-12:30pm Sat), in Palermo, offers Ashtanga, Hatha and Iyengar yoga at US$5 per class. Therapeutic massage and chakra balancing are also available.

Gay & Lesbian Travelers

¡Chao São Paulo! Buenos Aires is now South America's number-one gay destination – and for good reason. In 2002 the capital passed the continent's first ever gay and lesbian civil union laws allowing legal domestic partnerships; tourist offices hand out city-sponsored gay guides and maps; there are gay tango classes; and the gay clubbing and bar scene is vibrant. And hey, the tango was invented by men dancing with men, lest we forget.

As in most cities, the gay scene is dominated by men. Women, however, will find it easier to be affectionate in public, as it's not uncommon for women to walk hand in hand on the street. Outside gay venues, affection between men (including hand-holding) will draw unwanted attention.

Most gay clubs are in and around Barrio Norte and Palermo; see p67.

INFORMATION & ORGANIZATIONS
Comunidad Homosexual Argentina
(CHA; ☎ 4361-6382; www.cha.org.ar in Spanish) BA's longest running gay and lesbian organization.
Gay Guide (www.thegayguide.com.ar) Excellent resource aimed at foreigners; offers city tours.
Grupo Nexo (4, B3; ☎ 4375-0359; www .nexo.org in Spanish; 5th fl, Av Callao 339) Gay travel services and BA-specific links.
Lugar Gay de Buenos Aires (www.lugar gay.org) Gay B&B (p73) in San Telmo, and an excellent source of information even if you're not staying.
Pride Travel (6, E3; ☎ 5218-6556; www .pride-travel.com; Paraguay 523, 2E). Well-regarded queer travel agency.
Friendly Apartments (www.friendly apartments.com.ar) Apartment rental agency for gay visitors.

Health
IMMUNIZATIONS
No immunizations are required or needed to visit Buenos Aires.

PRECAUTIONS
The city's tap water is potable, though you may get mild stomach rumblings simply because the water is new to your system. Food preparation in restaurants is as clean as it is in countries like the US or Australia. The occasional exceptions are street and market food stalls, though they're almost always safe, especially if they're busy.

If you're traipsing around BA in the dead of summer, the heat and humidity can get to you, but there are plenty of cafés to stop for breaks.

MEDICAL SERVICES
Travel insurance is advisable to cover any medical treatment you may need while in Buenos Aires. English-speaking doctors are available by appointment at the private **Hospital Británico** (3, D3; ☎ 4304-1081; Perdriel 74; ☾ 24hr emergency) whose main facility is in Constitución. It has a more central **branch** (6, B3; ☎ 4812-0040; MT de Alvear 1573; ☾ 9am-5pm Mon-Fri) in Barrio Norte for consultations only.

DENTAL SERVICES
If you chip a tooth or need emergency treat-ment, head to **Hospital de Odontología Dr José Dueñas** (3, C3; ☎ 4983-0392/8983; Muñiz 15, Almagro). Consultations are free; bring your passport.

PHARMACIES
Pharmacies are everywhere in Buenos Aires. The biggest chain is **Farmacity** (www.farma city.com in Spanish) with some 60 branches throughout the city. Various branches are open 24 hours. If you visit a pharmacy and it's closed, the location of the nearest 24-hour pharmacy is usually posted in the window.

Holidays

January 1	Año Nuevo (New Year's Day)
March/April	Holy Thursday & Good Friday/Easter
May 1	Día de Trabajador (Labor Day)
May 25	Revolución de Mayo (May Revolution)
June 10	Día de las Malvinas (Malvinas Day)
June 20	Día de la Bandera (Flag Day)
July 9	Día de la Independencia (Independence Day)
August 17	Día de San Martín (date of San Martín's death)
October 12	Día de la Raza (Columbus Day)
November 10	Día de la Tradición (Day of Tradition)

| December 8 | Día de la Concepción Inmaculada (Immaculate Conception Day) |
| December 25 | (Navidad) Christmas Day |

Internet

Cybercafés, where you can access the Internet for about US$0.65 per hour, are everywhere. *Locutorios* (telephone kiosks) also often have computers with Internet access as well. Most hotels (and all top-end hotels) have direct dial-up or broadband lines in the rooms and/or have a business center with online access. Some charge for the service.

INTERNET SERVICE PROVIDERS

Alternativa Gratis (www.alternativa gratis.com.ar) Dial-up number is ☎ 5555-5555; *usuario* (user name) is 'alternativa'; *contraseña* (password) is 'gratis'.

Argentina.com (www.argentina.com) Dial-up number is ☎ 5254-5000; user name is 'argentina'; password is 'argentina'.

Ciber Gratis (www.cibergratis.com.ar) Dial-up number is ☎ 5670-0001; user name is 'ciber'; password is 'gratis'.

USEFUL WEBSITES

The Lonely Planet website (www.lonely planet.com) offers a speedy link to many of Buenos Aires' websites. Other useful sites include:

Buenos Aires Herald (www.buenosaires herald.com) Online portal of BA's English-language daily.

Clarín (www.clarin.com.ar, in Spanish) Argentina's largest-circulation daily.

La Nación (www.lanacion.com.ar, in Spanish) BA's oldest and most prestigious daily.

Latin American Network Information Center (www.lanic.utexas.edu/la /argentina) Extensive list of Argentine websites.

Secretaría de Turismo (www.turismo.gov .ar) The national tourist board's official website on Argentina.

Subsecretaría de Turismo (www.bue.gov .ar) The city's official tourism website.

What's Up Buenos Aires (www.whatsup buenosaires.com) Tune in to what's going down in BA.

Yes BA (www.yesba.org) Interesting mailing list (archived online) with entertainment, apartment rentals and more.

Lost Property

Unless your karma is due for a serious return, if you've lost something, it's likely gone for good. If you left something on a public bus, you can try calling the bus company (provided you remember which bus and which company you were riding with), but odds are you won't get it back.

Metric System

Argentina uses the metric system. Decimals are indicated with commas; thousands are indicated with points.

TEMPERATURE
°C = (°F - 32) ÷ 1.8
°F = (°C x 1.8) + 32

DISTANCE
1in = 2.54cm
1cm = 0.39in
1m = 3.3ft = 1.1yd
1ft = 0.3m
1km = 0.62 miles
1 mile = 1.6km

WEIGHT
1kg = 2.2lb
1lb = 0.45kg
1g = 0.04oz
1oz = 28g

VOLUME
1L = 0.26 US gallons
1 US gallon = 3.8L
1L = 0.22 imperial gallons
1 imperial gallon = 4.55L

Money
ATMS

Cajeros automáticos (ATMs) are located throughout the city. They're the best way to get cash, and can also be used for advances on major credit cards. Nearly all have instructions in English; most use Cirrus, Plus or Link systems. Make sure you have a four-digit PIN.

CREDIT CARDS

Many tourist services and most large hotels, finer dining establishments and shops accept Visa and MasterCard. When you're out shopping (especially in Palermo), prices may differ depending on whether you're paying *con tarjeta* (with a card) or *en efectivo* (in cash). Paying with a card can cost up to 10% more than with cash due to the *recargo* (surcharge) levied on most credit-card purchases.

Call the following for 24-hour assistance:
American Express (6, D2; ☎ 4312-1661; Arenales 707)
MasterCard (4, F4; ☎ 4348-7070; Perú 151)
Visa (4, C2; ☎ 4379-3400; Av Corrientes 1437)

CURRENCY

Argentina's currency is the peso (denoted as AR\$ when used in this book). Bills come in denominations of two, five, 10, 20, 50 and 100 pesos. One peso equals 100 centavos; coins come in denominations of five, 10, 25 and 50 centavos, and one peso. Changing a 50 or 100 peso bill at kiosks or smaller businesses is nearly always impossible, so change it whenever the chance arises in restaurants or supermarkets.

MONEYCHANGERS

Banks will exchange cash, but usually have more limited hours than *casas de cambio* (exchange houses). Both are common throughout the center, and there's a *casa de cambio* at Ezeiza airport. A good, central *casa de cambio* is **Alhec** (6, D3; ☎ 4316-5000; Paraguay 641; ☽ 10am-4:30pm Mon-Fri), and there are many others in the Microcentro. Rates are usually very similar.

TRAVELER'S CHECKS

Leave them at home – hardly anyone accepts them. If you do need to cash traveler's checks, do so at banks or *casas de cambio*, and expect a hefty surcharge. Cash American Express checks without commission at **American Express** (6, D2; ☎ 4312-1661; Arenales 707; ☽ 10am-3pm Mon-Fri).

Newspapers & Magazines

The capital's biggest daily newspapers are *Clarín* and *La Nación*. Founded in 1876, the *Buenos Aires Herald* is the city's English-language daily. For sports pick up *Olé*. All are sold at newspaper kiosks. *Llegás* is a free culture and entertainment weekly and the best source for what's up in BA; pick up a copy at tourist offices, cultural centers, bars and shops. For opinionated leftist news, pick up the excellent *Pagina 12*. *Hecho en Buenos Aires* is the local street sheet, published to benefit the folks who peddle them.

Photography & Video

Unless you need pro development, process your photos *before* returning home. You'll save heaps. Kodak and Agfa stores offering one-hour development (which usually means three to six hours) are everywhere; the latter usually do better work and offer better paper selections. Pro film is hard to find, but standard print film is readily available and costs about US\$3 to US\$5 per roll. E-6 (slide) film is hard to come by. **Cosentino** (4, E3; 4328-3290; Bartolomé Mitre 845) has the best selection of film (including E-6 and black-and-white) and photography supplies in town. Argentina uses PAL-N or PAL-CN video systems. At most cybercafés you can have your photos downloaded and burned to a CD. Some have CD burners on their public computers so you can do it yourself.

Post

Correo Argentino (www.correoargentino.com.ar in Spanish), the privatized national postal service, has gotten more reliable over the years but mail still occasionally gets waylaid. Its main office is the **Correo Central** (4, H2; ☎ 4894-9191; Av Sarmiento 151; ☽ 8am-8pm Mon-Fri, 9am-1pm Sat), inside the Palacio de Correos (p25), which fills an entire city block. No need to wait in line here though; numerous branch offices are scattered throughout the city, often as part of smaller stores. Look for the Correo Argentino sign.

POSTAL RATES
International letters and postcards under 20g cost US$1.35; a letter over 20g costs US$3.20. Certified letters to the US cost US$4.45 for up to 100g, and US$4.75 to the rest of the world. For essential overseas mail, send it *certificado* (certified).

Radio
No hard chords on the car radio here, but: FM 92.7 plays tango 24/7, FM 92.3 is Argentine folk and FM 98.3 kicks out non-stop *rock nacional* (Argentine rock). FM 97.1 broadcasts BBC in English from noon to 5pm. Get your electronic dance kicks on FM 95.1, which plays electronica by night. La Colifata (The Crazy One) at FM 100.1 runs from 3pm to 7:30pm Saturday; it's operated by institutionalized psychiatric patients.

Telephone
Two companies, Telecom and Telefónica, split the city's telephone services. The easiest way to make a local phone call is to find a *locutorio* (small telephone office), where you call from a private cabin and pay at the register when you're through. There's a *locutorio* on practically every other block, they cost about the same as street phones, are much quieter and you won't run out of coins. Most *locutorios* are supplied with phone books.

CELL PHONES
The main cell-phone systems are CDMA and TDMA. It's now possible to use a tri-band GSM world cell phone in BA. This is a fast-changing field so take a look at www .kropla.com or do an Internet search on GSM cell phones for the myriad of products on the market.

COUNTRY & CITY CODES
Argentina's country code is ☎ 54. The *característica* (area code) for Buenos Aires is ☎ 011, but drop the zero if calling from abroad. All telephone numbers in the Greater Buenos Aires area have eight digits. Cell-phone numbers are always preceded by '15,' which you must dial unless calling from another cell phone. Toll-free numbers begin with ☎ 0-800 or ☎ 0-810.

PHONECARDS
Tarjetas telefónicas (phone cards) are sold at most kiosks and *locutorios* and can be used for pay phones. You can use them to make local, national and international calls from a fixed line; you can't use them from cell phones or at most *locutorios*. Calling cards offer the best international rates and can be used from most hotel phones and all private lines.

USEFUL PHONE NUMBERS
Directory Assistance (☎ 110)
International Direct Dial Code (☎ 00 + country code)
International Operator (☎ 000)
Telecom/Telefónica Service (☎ 112)
Time (☎ 113)

Television
Most hotel rooms have cable and/or satellite TV. Canal 7 is the only state-run TV channel, with loads of culture and music programs.

Time
Buenos Aires is three hours behind GMT/UTC and does not practice daylight-savings time.

Tipping
Tip 8% to 10% on restaurant tabs even when a *cubierto* (silverware charge) is included. Bartenders are occasionally tipped, and they often ring a bar bell when it happens. Leave cab drivers the small change.

Toilets

Public toilets are hard to find. Make use of McToilets when you see fast-food chains. Shopping centers and busy cafés are other good places to relieve yourself.

Tourist Information

The **Secretaría de Turismo de la Nación** (6, D2; ☎ 4312-2232; www.turismo.gov.ar; Av Santa Fe 883; ☺ 9am-5pm weekdays) has information on BA and Argentina. The **Comisaría del Turista** (Tourist Police; 4, G2; ☎ 4346-5748, 0-800-999-5000; turista@ policiafederal.gov.ar; Av Corrientes 436; ☺ 24hr) provides interpreters and helps crime victims.

Several of the city's tourist kiosks do not have telephones, but there's a toll-free **tourist information line** (☎ 0-800-555-0016; ☺ 8am-8pm). Tourist kiosks:

Aeroparque airport (3, C1; ☎ 4773-9805; ☺ 8am-8pm).

Ezeiza airport (☎ 4480-0224; ☺ 8am-8pm)

Microcentro (4, F3; cnr Florida & Diagonal Roque Sáenz Peña; ☺ 9am-6pm Mon-Sat)

Puerto Madero (4, H1; Puerto Madero at Dique 4; ☎ 4313-0187; ☺ 11am-6pm Mon-Fri, 11am-7pm Sat)

Recoleta (2, C2; Av Quintana 596; ☺ 10:30am-6:30pm Mon-Fri, 10am-7pm Sat-Sun)

Retiro (6, D2; MT de Alvear; ☺ 10am-7pm)

Retiro bus station (3, D2; ☎ 4311-0528; ste 83, 2nd fl, Av Ramos Mejía 1680; ☺ 7:30am-1pm Mon-Sat)

San Telmo (5, C2; Defensa 1250; ☺ 11am-5pm Mon-Fri, 11am-7pm Sat & Sun)

Women Travelers

Buenos Aires is a modern and sophisticated city, and women travelers – even those traveling alone – should not encounter many difficulties. Men do pay more overt attention to women, however, and some feel the need to comment on a woman's attractiveness. Comments come in the form of whistles or *piropos* (compliments), which many Argentine men consider an art. Much as you may want to kick 'em where it counts, the best thing to do is to completely ignore it. When standing on the street looking at a map, the average wait-time for a man to stop to offer directions is about one minute, 12 seconds.

LANGUAGE

Argentine Spanish, called *castellano,* is heavily influence by Italian, especially in Buenos Aires. Argentines use the second-person *voseo (vos)* instead of the *tú* form used in the rest of Latin America. Porteños further complicate the language with *lunfardo,* the complex slang rooted in Italian and the early tango underground. *Lunfardo* words you're bound to hear include *'che'* (dude), *'piola'* (cool), *'pucho'* (cigarette), *'morfar'* (to eat), *'bondi'* (bus). *'Boludo'* (jerk, asshole, idiot) is a favorite insult, often used in a friendly fashion. Lonely Planet's *Latin American Spanish Phrasebook* is handy to have along.

Basics

Good morning.	Buenos días.
Good afternoon.	Buenas tardes.
Hi!	¡Hola!
Bye!	¡Chau!
Please.	Por favor.
Thank you (very much).	(Muchas) Gracias.
Yes	Sí.
No.	No.
Excuse me. (to get past)	Permiso.
Sorry!	¡Perdón!
Pardon? (as in 'What did you say?')	¿Cómo?/¿Qué?
Do you speak English?	¿Hablá inglés?
Does anyone speak English?	¿Hay alguien que hable inglés?
Do you understand? (informal)	¿Me entendés?
Yes, I understand.	Sí, entiendo.
No, I don't understand.	No, no entiendo.

Index

See also separate Indexes for Eating (p93), Sleeping (p95), Shopping (p94) and Sights with map references (p94).

FEATURES

Persicco	*Eating*
Club Niceto	*Entertainment*
Acabar	*Drinking*
Café Tortino	*Café*
Teatro Colón	*Highlights*
Amor Latino	*Shopping*
Museo Evita	*Sights/Activities*
Malabia House	*Sleeping*

AREAS

	Beach, Desert
	Building
	Land
	Mall
	Other Area
	Park/Cemetery
	Sports
	Urban

HYDROGRAPHY

	River, Creek
	Intermittent River
	Canal
	Swamp
	Water

BOUNDARIES

	State, Provincial
	Regional, Suburb
	Ancient Wall

ROUTES

	Tollway
	Freeway
	Primary Road
	Secondary Road
	Tertiary Road
	Lane
	Under Construction
	One-Way Street
	Unsealed Road
	Mall/Steps
	Tunnel
	Walking Path
	Walking Trail/Track
	Pedestrian Overpass
	Walking Tour

TRANSPORT

	Airport, Airfield
	Bus Route
	Cycling, Bicycle Path
	Ferry
	General Transport
	Monorail
	Rail
	Subte
	Taxi Rank
	Tram

SYMBOLS

	Bank, ATM
	Buddhist
	Castle, Fortress
	Christian
	Diving, Snorkeling
	Embassy, Consulate
	Hospital, Clinic
	Information
	Internet Access
	Islamic
	Jewish
	Lighthouse
	Lookout
	Monument
	Mountain, Volcano
	National Park
	Parking Area
	Petrol Station
	Picnic Area
	Point of Interest
	Police Station
	Post Office
	Ruin
	Telephone
	Toilets
	Zoo, Bird Sanctuary
	Waterfall

From **bland** To *Grand*

The Ultimate Sauce, Salsa & Chutney Cookbook!

From **bland**
To
Grand

The Ultimate Sauce, Salsa
& Chutney Cookbook!

Printed in China
Copyright © 2012 KitchenAdvance
ISBN 978-1-938653-08-7

Table of *Contents*

Salsas

Sauces

SousVide Suggestions 95

Introduction

Chutneys date as far back as 500BC, and have been used to spice up food and excite the palate ever since. Though once thought to be reserved for more ethnic cuisines, our ever-changing and evolving world food cultures have embraced chutneys, relishes, salsas, and other sauces in more everyday cooking. In this book we show you just how easy and versatile these condiments truly are.

Everyday at-home cooks used to believe that they were not capable of creating meals as exciting and gourmet as the chefs in four-star restaurants, but today all the tools and secrets available to those chefs are available to you. In this book we will not only share the secrets of unique flavor combinations, but also tips for using the revolutionary sous vide cooking technique, made simple by AquaChef. The recipes found in this book are the perfect compliment to the delicious and fool-proof dishes cooked with the AquaChef. With the knowledge of sous vide cooking and the recipes for exciting chutneys, salsas and sauces, your at-home cooking will be four-star delicious!

Sous Vide Application

AquaChef is one of the best and most simple implementations of sous vide cooking yet! With the AquaChef meats, fish, vegetables and other dishes come out perfect every time. Some people find the revolutionary results of the AquaChef sous vide cooking to be more than enough delicious to last an entire meal, but the more adventurous want more.

One of the best things about cooking with the AquaChef is that your main dishes are so quick and simple that it allows you extra time to further spice up your meals. In this book we offer an enormous variety of recipes for chutneys, relishes, salsas and other sauces that can be prepared at almost any time and combined with your AquaChef dishes to create one unbelievable meal.

Whether you decide to infuse your chicken breast with the exotic flavors of a chutney by cooking them together in the AquaChef, or you want to add a fresh salsa atop a perfectly cooked fish fillet, these recipes, along with the simplicity of the AquaChef, make your options almost endless.

The last chapter offers a few great sous vide recipes for your AquaChef that are the perfect match to many of these delicious chutneys, relishes, salsas, and sauces.

Chutneys/ Relishes

Chutneys were invented to help mask the flavors of spoiled fruits and vegetables. Today, with refrigeration and freezing, we no longer have that problem, making these condiments a fantastic way to explore and add exciting and unique flavor and texture combinations to your favorite dishes.

Made from any number of ingredients, chutneys normally contain some mixture of spices and vegetables and/or fruits. Though often chunky, chutneys can vary in texture, being anywhere from smooth and fine and even dry, to wet and thick. How they are prepared is also something that differs from recipe to recipe. Many of the ingredients can be chopped, or ground in a mortar and pestle. Food processors also work great in preparing chutneys, saving time in the preparation.

Though there are many classic chutney recipes, it is a condiment that can be played and experimented with, and you will find an endless amount of combinations and flavors to compliment your favorite dishes. Whether you like a sweet or spicy chutney, you are guaranteed to enjoy the taste and texture it can add to a dish.

Relishes are similar to chutneys, but do stand on their own. Cooked or pickled, a relish mainly contains a chopped fruit or vegetable, anywhere from fine to coarse. Like chutneys, with a relish you can explore many types of recipes with endless flavor and texture combinations.

Apple Spice *Chutney*

---

suggested use

This chutney works best with roast chicken, but is also great with pork.

---

yields: 2 cups

2 *large* Northern Spy *or other tart apples, peeled & chopped*
½ *cup* onion, chopped
¼ *cup* red wine vinegar
¼ *cup* brown sugar
1 *tbsp* orange zest
1 *tbsp* ginger, minced
½ *tsp* allspice

Place all ingredients in a saucepan and bring to a boil over medium heat, stirring well. Lower heat and simmer for 40 minutes, covered. Remove lid and continue to simmer for a few minutes longer to reduce liquid. Let cool. Cover and refrigerate for up to 2 weeks.

Apple & Fig
Chutney

---

suggested use

This chutney works great with any pork dish.

---

yields: 2 cups

*2 apples, peeled,
cored & sliced
12 oz dried figs,
chopped
1 2" stick cinnamon
1 tbsp lemon juice
1 cup apple cider vinegar*

Heat all ingredients in a large saucepan over medium heat until boiling. Turn down heat to a high simmer. Simmer slowly until apples start to break apart and figs have softened, approximately 45 minutes to 1 hour.

Apricot

suggested use

Spoon this over slices of pork roast or serve with pork chops. It is also great with chicken and turkey breasts.

yields: 3 cups

2½ lbs apricots, quartered
1 lb red onions, diced
2 cups golden raisins
1 lb brown sugar
2 cups apple cider vinegar
1 tsp chili powder
2 tsp yellow mustard seeds
1 tsp salt
½ tsp turmeric
½ tsp cinnamon

Place apricots, onion, raisins, sugar, vinegar, chili powder, mustard seeds, salt, turmeric and cinnamon in a 4-quart saucepan. Bring to a boil over medium heat. Lower heat and simmer, stirring frequently, 45 to 60 minutes or until the mixture has thickened to a light syrup. Cool to room temperature. Refrigerate up to 3 weeks.

Coconut

Chutney

yields: 2½ cups

1 *tbsp vegetable oil*
4 *tbsp coconut, grated*
2 *tsp chickpeas, roasted*
1" *piece ginger, peeled &*
chopped
4 *tbsp cilantro, chopped*
2 *jalapeños, chopped*
1 *tsp mustard seeds*
to taste salt

Heat the vegetable oil in a small saucepan, add mustard seeds and sauté until they sputter a bit and are fragrant. Remove from heat. Add mustard seeds to the rest of the ingredients in the bowl of a food processor, processing until almost smooth. Add a small amount of water if mixture is too thick. Add salt to taste.

Cranberry Apple

Chutney

---

suggested use

This relish is a nice change from the traditional cranberry sauce. It works well with turkey, chicken and pork.

---

yields: 1½ cups

12 oz cranberries (fresh or frozen)
1 apple, peeled & diced
½ pear, peeled & diced
½ cup dried cranberries
¾ cup sugar
¼ cup orange juice
½ tsp orange zest
1 pinch nutmeg
2 tbsp Grand Marnier or other orange liqueur

Place cranberries, apple, pear, dried cranberries, sugar, orange juice and zest, and nutmeg in a 4-quart saucepan. Bring mixture to a boil. Lower heat and simmer, uncovered, stirring frequently, until fruit is tender and mixture thickens a bit, about 30 to 45 minutes. Cool slightly and stir in the liqueur. Chill for 2 hours. Store in refrigerator for up to 1 week.

Cranberry *Chutney*

suggested use

Serve this chutney with turkey, or try it with chicken or pork, or even spooned over a soft cheese, like brie.

yields: 3 cups

12 oz *cranberries (fresh or frozen)*
2 *apples, peeled & diced*
¾ *cup onion, diced*
4 *cloves garlic, minced*
2 *tbsp ginger, minced*
¾ *cup dark raisins*
1 *cup sugar*
1 *cup red wine or raspberry vinegar*
½ *tsp salt*

Place all ingredients in a saucepan and bring to a boil over medium heat, stirring well. Lower heat and simmer for 40 minutes, covered. Remove lid and continue to simmer for a few minutes longer to reduce liquid. Let cool. Cover and refrigerate for up to 2 weeks.

Cranberry Mango

---

suggested use

This relish is perfect with roast turkey, this is also great with any other light meat, such as chicken.

---

yields: 2½ cups

1 lb (about 2) mangoes
2 cups cranberries
(fresh, not frozen)
½ medium orange, unpeeled
& cubed
½ cup sugar

Peel mangoes and cut into cubes. Place mango, cranberries and orange in the food processor. Pulse to coarsely chop. Add sugar and pulse to combine. Do not puree. Let relish stand 30 minutes before serving. Refrigerate up to 3 days.

Crunchy Corn
Chutney

---

suggested use

Serve for a Southwestern flavor on chicken, or with grilled ribs.

---

yields: 4 cups

2 *cups fresh corn kernels*
2 *cups jicama, peeled*
& diced
½ *cup red bell pepper,*
diced
½ *cup green bell pepper,*
diced
1 *jalapeño, seeded &*
minced
½ *cup champagne vinegar*
2 *tbsp vegetable oil*
2 *tbsp sugar*
3 *tbsp cilantro,*
chopped
2 *tsp ground cumin*
¼ *tsp pepper*
¼ *tsp salt*

Place corn kernels, jicama, red and green peppers and the jalapeño in a large bowl. Toss to combine. Add the vinegar, oil, sugar, cilantro, cumin, pepper and salt. Toss to combine thoroughly. Chill for at least 2 hours. Drain before serving or serve with a slotted spoon. Keeps for one week.

Papaya
Chutney

suggested use

This sweet chutney works well with lean meats, or with a cheese appetizer.

yields: 2 cups

1½ lbs papaya, peeled, seeded & chopped
1 large apple, peeled & chopped
1 cup onion, chopped
½ cup red bell pepper, chopped
¼ cup dark raisins
¼ cup golden raisins
½ cup sugar
½ cup cider vinegar
½ tsp salt
¾ tsp mustard seeds
¼ tsp red pepper flakes, crushed
1 tbsp crystallized ginger
2 tbsp vegetable oil

Heat vegetable oil over a medium flame in a 3-quart saucepan. Add mustard seeds and red pepper flakes. Stir until fragrant, 30-60 seconds. Add the rest of the ingredients and bring to a boil over medium heat. Continue to cook uncovered for 30 to 40 minutes, stirring occasionally, until fruit is tender and mixture has thickened.

Peach & Cherry
Chutney

suggested use

This chutney works well with shrimp, pork or chicken.

yields: 2½ cups

3 peaches, peeled & diced
1 cup dried cherries
½ cup onion, chopped
¼ cup maple syrup
1 cup red wine or raspberry vinegar
¼ tsp salt
¼ tsp pepper
¼ cup mint, chopped

Place peaches, cherries, onion, maple syrup, vinegar, salt and pepper in a 3-quart saucepan and bring to a boil over medium heat. Lower heat and simmer for 15 minutes. Add the mint and continue to cook for 5 to 10 minutes or until the mixture has thickened slightly. Cool to room temperature and store in the refrigerator up to 2 weeks.

Pear & Walnut

Chutney

---

suggested use

This chutney is great with pork or lamb kabobs.

---

yields: 2½ cups

3 *cups* pears, diced
& peeled
1 *small* onion, diced
1 *cup* walnuts, coarsely
chopped
2 *tbsp* ginger,
minced
1 *cup* cider vinegar
½ *cup* brown sugar
¼ *tsp* salt

Place pears, onion, walnuts, ginger, vinegar, sugar and salt in a 3-quart saucepan. Bring to a boil over medium heat. Lower heat and simmer for 15-20 minutes or until fruit is tender and mixture has thickened slightly. Let cool to room temperature. Refrigerate up to 2 weeks.

Pineapple

Chutney

suggested use

This tart and sweet chutney is great with fish, or shrimp.

yields: 4 cups

½ pineapple, peeled & diced
1 apple, peeled & diced
1 small onion, diced
1 cup cider vinegar
½ cup brown sugar
1 tbsp ginger, minced
4 cloves garlic, minced
¼ tsp pepper
¼ tsp salt
1 pinch cayenne pepper
1 tbsp cilantro, chopped

Place the pineapple, apple, onion, vinegar, brown sugar, ginger, garlic, pepper and salt in a 4-quart saucepan. Bring to a boil over medium heat. Lower heat and simmer for 45 minutes or until fruit is tender and mixture has a jam-like texture. Stir in cayenne and cilantro. Let cool to room temperature. Store in the refrigerator up to 2 weeks.

Rhubarb
Chutney

This tart and sweet chutney works well with pork tenderloin or as a sauce for pork chops.

yields: 3 cups

¾ *cup sugar*
½ *cup cider vinegar*
1 *tbsp ginger, minced*
1 *tbsp garlic, minced*
1 *tsp ground cumin*
½ *tsp ground cloves*
¼ *tsp red pepper flakes, crushed*
1½ *lbs rhubarb, cut into ½" cubes*
½ *cup red onion, chopped*
¼ *cup golden raisins*

Place the sugar, vinegar, ginger, garlic, cumin, cloves, red pepper flakes, and red onion in a 4-quart saucepan and bring to a boil over medium heat. Add rhubarb and raisins. Increase the heat to medium high and cook until rhubarb is just tender, but not falling apart, and mixture thickens slightly, about 5 minutes. Cool to room temperature. Refrigerate 1 day before using.

Roast Lemon

Chutney

suggested use

This chutney is great with fresh ricotta or goat cheese, for instance on a bruschetta.

yields: 1½ cups

¼ *cup* shallots, minced
3 *small* meyer lemons
¼ *cup* olive oil
(extra for brushing lemons when cooking)
1 *tbsp* honey
to taste kosher/sea salt
to taste black pepper, freshly ground

Heat the oven to 400°F. Line a baking sheet with parchment paper. Slice off each end of two of the lemons. Slice them into ¼-inch-thick rounds, removing seeds as you slice. Arrange the lemons on the baking sheet and brush both sides with oil. Roast the lemons, turning every 5 minutes, until tender, 20 to 25 minutes (do not let the lemons brown in more than a few spots and do not let them dry out). Transfer the roasted lemons to a food processor. Add the shallots and honey. Pulse until the lemon is chopped. Add the juice from half the remaining lemon and the olive oil. Pulse until the chutney is somewhat smooth and creamy, with only small chunks remaining. Season with salt and pepper to taste, adding more honey as necessary. Cool to room temperature before serving.

Spiced Apple

---

suggested use

Serve this beside a spice-crusted and roasted pork loin or tenderloin.

---

yields: 2½ cups

3 *cups granny smith apples, peeled & chopped*
½ *cup onions, chopped*
½ *cup red bell pepper, chopped*
½ *cup golden raisins*
½ *cup dark raisins*
2 *tsp yellow mustard seeds*
1 *tsp ground ginger*
½ *tsp ground cinnamon*
½ *tsp salt*
1 *cup cider vinegar*
½ *cup brown sugar*

Place apples, onion, red pepper, raisins, mustard seeds, spices, salt, vinegar and sugar in a 3-quart saucepan and bring to a boil over medium heat. Lower heat and simmer for 20 to 30 minutes or until the apples are tender and the mixture has a jam-like consistency. Cool to room temperature. Store in the refrigerator for up to 2 weeks.

Spiced Apricot
Chutney

suggested use

This spiced apricot chutney is delicious served with pork, or another savory rich meat.

yields: 2 cups

2 *cups dried apricots,*
finely chopped
¼ *cup sugar*
¼ *cup honey*
½ *tsp cinnamon*
¼ *tsp ground nutmeg*
¼ *tsp ground cloves*
½ *cup water*

Place apricots, water, sugar, honey, cinnamon, nutmeg and cloves in a medium saucepan. Bring to a simmer, stirring until sugar dissolves. Continue to simmer for 5 minutes. Stir in apricots and heat through, another 2 or 3 minutes.

Spicy Mango
Chutney

---

suggested use

This sweet chutney is great with roasted meats.

---

yields: 2½ cups

3 cups mango, diced
1 apple, peeled
& diced
1 small onion, diced
½ cup red bell pepper, diced
1 red jalapeño, seeded
& minced
1 clove garlic, minced
½ cup brown sugar
1 cup white wine vinegar
½ tsp salt
¼ tsp freshly ground pepper
1 pinch cayenne pepper
2 tbsp ginger, minced

Place mango, apple, onion, red pepper, red chili, garlic, brown sugar, vinegar, salt and pepper in a 3-quart saucepan. Bring to boil over medium heat. Simmer for 20-30 minutes or until fruit is tender and mixture has thickened slightly. Stir in cayenne and ginger. Let cool to room temperature. Refrigerate up to 2 weeks.

Spicy Onion

Chutney

Serve this with a pork loin or pork tenderloin.

yields: 2 cups

1¼ lbs (about 4 cups)
red onions, chopped
3 tbsp olive oil
3 jalapeño chilies,
seeded & minced
2 tbsp honey
4 tbsp red wine vinegar
¼ cup water

Place the onion and olive oil in a large skillet and cook until softened, about 10 minutes. Season with salt and pepper. Add the jalapeño and cook 1 minute more. Add vinegar and honey and cook until almost all liquid is evaporated. Add the water and simmer, stirring often until slightly thickened and very tender, about 10 minutes. Serve immediately or refrigerate up to 2 days. Reheat before serving.

Tamarind

Chutney

---

suggested use

This sweet, indian-spiced chutney will go well with kabobs or a grilled fish.

---

yields: 1¼ cups

1 *tbsp* vegetable oil
1 *tsp* cumin seeds
1 *tsp* ground ginger
½ *tsp* cayenne pepper
½ *tsp* fennel seeds
½ *tsp* garam masala
1½ *cups* water
½ *cup* white sugar
3 *tbsp* tamarind paste

Heat oil in a large saucepan over medium heat. Add the cumin seeds, ginger, cayenne pepper, fennel seeds, and garam masala. Cook and stir for about 2 minutes to release the flavors. Stir the water into the pan along with the sugar and tamarind paste. Bring to a boil, then simmer over low heat until the mixture turns dark brown and is thick enough to coat the back of a metal spoon, approximately 20-30 minutes. The sauce will thicken as it cools.

Tomato

Chutney

---

suggested use

Serve this with a beef roast or steak, or spread on a roast beef sandwich.

---

yields: 1½ cups

1 lb tomatoes, peeled,
seeded & diced
¾ cup red bell pepper,
diced
½ cup red wine vinegar
¾ cup cider vinegar
½ cup sugar
1 tsp salt
2 tsp yellow mustard seeds
½ tsp pepper, freshly
ground
½ tsp red pepper flakes,
crushed
¾ cup green onions,
chopped

Set aside tomatoes and red bell pepper. Place both vinegars, sugar, salt, mustard seeds, pepper and red pepper flakes in a 3-quart saucepan. Bring to a boil over medium high heat. Stir in the tomatoes, red bell pepper and green onions. Lower heat and simmer 1 hour or until thickened and reduced to about 1½ cups. Cool to room temperature. Refrigerate up to 2 weeks.

Tropical
Chutney

---

suggested use

*This tropical spiced chutney works
well with grilled chicken or seafood.*

---

yields: 4 cups

2 *tbsp* olive oil
1 *tsp* red pepper flakes,
crushed
1 *large* sweet onion,
finely chopped
2 *tbsp* ginger root,
peeled & minced
1 *yellow* bell pepper,
diced
3 *large* ripe mangoes,
peeled & diced
1 *small* pineapple,
peeled & diced
¼ *cup* brown sugar
1 *tbsp* curry powder
¼ *cup* apple cider vinegar
¼ *cup* apple juice

Heat the oil in a very large saucepan over medium-low heat. Stir in the pepper flakes and cook 60 seconds, then stir in the onion. Reduce the heat to low, and cook, stirring occasionally until the onions have softened and are translucent, about 15 minutes. Increase the heat to medium, and stir in the ginger and yellow bell pepper. Cook and stir until the ginger is fragrant, 2 to 3 minutes. Stir in the remaining ingredients. Bring to a simmer, and cook for 30 minutes, stirring occasionally. Cool to room temperature before using.

Two Cherry
Chutney

---

suggested use

Serve with pork chops, pork tenderloin, seared duck breasts, or baked chicken.

---

yields: 3 cups

3 *tbsp olive oil*
2 *tbsp shallots, minced*
(can substitute
with red onion)
1 *cup tart cherries,*
fresh & pitted,
roughly chopped
1 *cup sweet cherries,*
fresh & pitted,
roughly chopped
½ *cup walnuts,*
chopped
1 *tsp rosemary,*
minced
¼ *cup port or kirsch*
2 *tbsp honey*
¼ *tsp black pepper*
to taste salt

Sauté shallots in olive oil over medium heat until soft and translucent. Add rosemary, walnuts and cherries, turn down heat to low and stir until cherries are soft. Add pepper and salt to taste. Pour in port or kirsch and the honey. Turn up heat to medium and boil very slowly until liquid has a syrupy texture. Remove from heat and let cool.

Winter Fruit
Chutney

suggested use

This chutney is great with a roast bird, or other wintry meat, such as a pork roast.

yields: 2½ cups

½ *orange*
1½ *cups dry white wine*
¼ *cup sugar*
1 *tbsp lemon juice*
1 *cinnamon stick*
1 *bay leaf*
1½ *tsp coriander seeds*
1½ *tsp whole black*
peppercorns
½ *cup dried cranberries*
½ *cup dried figs,*
coarsely chopped
¼ *cup dark raisins*
1½ *tbsp ginger,*
minced
½ *lb apples, peeled*
& diced

Remove pith from orange, separate segments from membranes. Place white wine, sugar, lemon juice, cinnamon stick, bay leaf, coriander seeds, peppercorns in a 4-quart saucepan. Cover, bring to a boil. Simmer 15 minutes. Strain mixture, discard solids. Return liquid to saucepan, add cranberries, figs, raisins, ginger. Cover, simmer until fruit is tender, about 10 minutes. Add apples, simmer 15 minutes. Stir in reserved orange segments. Cool to room temperature. Refrigerate up to 1 week.

Salsas

Salsas have been around since the Aztecs combined chilies with tomatoes, though the actual term "salsa" was in fact coined by the Spanish conquistadores. Tomatoes and tomatillos are found in Peru, Ecuador, and Colombia, and Aztecs would combine them with chillies, squash seeds, beans, and other ingredients, and grind, mix and chop them into delicious mixes.

From then on the delicious and often spicy flavor combinations started spreading all over the world. By the 1800's salsas and hot sauces were being bottled and written about in the United States. Over the years, hot sauces were manufactured and often referred to as salsas, but in 1941 La Victoria Sales Company manufactured and sold the first true salsa in the United States. In the late 1980's salsa sales grew 79%, and by the 1990's, the sale of salsa overtook the previous American favorite, ketchup.

If you're not as familiar with cooking salsas as you are with other sauces, or are looking to expand your knowledge on the many variations, we hope this chapter brings you fun and excitement in your kitchen and on your plate!

Avocado
Salsa

This is great with a roast chicken, fish, or even with grilled vegetables.

yields: 2½ cups

*2 **medium** avocadoes, diced*
*½ **cup** tomato, diced*
*½ **cup** red onion, diced*
*2 **tbsp** cilantro, chopped*
*1 **clove** garlic, minced*
*1 **tbsp** lime juice*
1 serrano chili, minced
*½ **tsp** salt*

Toss the avocado with the tomato, red onion, cilantro, garlic, lime juice, chili and salt. Use within 8 hours.

Bean & Corn

Salsa

---

suggested use

This salsa is almost like a salad. Eat it with chicken or grilled fish.

---

yields: 3 cups

3 tomatoes, diced
1 to 2 jalapeño chilies, seeded & minced
1½ cup corn kernels
¾ cup can black beans, drained & rinsed
¼ cup red onion, diced
1 tbsp cilantro, minced
1 tbsp lime juice
1 tsp ground cumin
¼ tsp salt
¼ tsp cayenne pepper

Place tomatoes, jalapeño, corn, black beans, red onion and cilantro in a medium bowl. Toss with lime juice, cumin, hot sauce, salt and cayenne pepper. Serve immediately or refrigerate up to 2 days.

Black Bean

Salsa

---

suggested use

This bean salsa is great with a grilled steak, chicken, or fish.

---

yields: 2 cups

1 15 oz can black beans, drained & rinsed
1 large orange
¼ cup red bell pepper, diced
¼ cup green onions, sliced
¼ cup lime juice
2 tbsp vegetable oil
½ tsp salt

Place black beans in a medium bowl. Peel orange and cut into ½ inch pieces. Add orange to beans along with green onions, bell pepper, lime juice and oil. Toss gently to combine. Season with salt.

Italian
Salsa

---

suggested use

Use this as the topping for bruschetta, or on fish or chicken.

---

yields: 2 cups

4 *tomatoes, seeded*
& finely diced
4 *cloves garlic, minced*
2 *tbsp olive oil*
¼ *cup basil, thinly sliced*
½ *tsp salt*
¼ *tsp freshly ground pepper*

Place the tomatoes in a medium bowl and toss in the garlic, olive oil, basil, salt and pepper. Let stand at room temperature 30 to 60 minutes and serve.

Mango Cilantro
Salsa

This sweet salsa is great with blackened chicken or fish, or with a light meat.

yields: 1½ cups

2 mangoes, peeled
& diced
¼ cup red onion,
finely chopped
3 tbsp cilantro, chopped
2 tbsp lime juice
2 tbsp orange juice
½ tsp salt
¼ tsp freshly ground pepper

Place mango in a medium bowl. Gently toss in the red onion, cilantro, lime juice, orange juice, salt and pepper. Set aside to marinate for up to 3 hours.

Mild Chili

Salsa

---

suggested use

This mild yet flavorful cooked salsa is great with chicken or served with chips.

---

yields: 2 cups

½ *cup white onion,*
chopped
1 *clove garlic, minced*
1 *tbsp olive oil*
½ *jalapeño, finely*
chopped
2 *large tomatoes, peeled,*
seeded & chopped
½ *tsp salt*
1 *tbsp cilantro,*
chopped

Cook the onion and garlic in the oil in a medium skillet over medium heat. Add the chilies and tomatoes and simmer for 15 minutes. Add salt and stir in cilantro. Let cool.

Papaya

---

suggested use

This fresh salsa is great with cheese quesadillas or with a chicken or fish.

---

yields: 2½ cups

1 *tbsp vegetable oil*
½ *cup red onion, chopped*
½ *cup red bell pepper, chopped*
½ *tsp serrano chili, finely chopped*
2 *tbsp cilantro, minced*
2 *tbsp lime juice*
2 *cups papaya, diced*

Place the onion, red bell pepper and chili into a medium bowl. Stir in the cilantro, lime juice and papaya. Cover and refrigerate until chilled, about 2 hours.

Peach

Salsa

Serve this summery salsa with chicken or fish kabobs, or shrimp. It is also good with a smoky marinated and grilled pork tenderloin.

yields: 3 cups

1½ *lbs peaches*
¼ *cup red bell pepper, finely diced*
¼ *cup red onion, chopped*
¼ *cup raspberry vinegar*
2 *tbsp vegetable oil*
1 *to* 2 *jalapeño chilies, seeded & minced*
1 *tbsp cilantro, minced*

Peel peaches and coarsely chop. Toss peaches with red bell pepper, red onion, vinegar, oil, jalapeño chilies, and cilantro in a medium bowl. Let sit for up to 2 hours before serving. Store up to 1 week in the refrigerator.

Rooster's Beak

Salsa

---

suggested use

*This Mexican salsa, widely known as "pico de gallo"
or "salsa fresca," must be used quickly. Serve it with a
Southwestern style meat or fish.*

---

yields: 2 cups

2 tomatoes, diced
*2 long Anaheim chilies, seeded
& diced*
1 jalapeño, seeded & diced
2 green onions, chopped
1 tbsp lime juice
1 clove garlic, minced
2 tbsp cilantro, chopped
½ tsp salt

Place the tomatoes, chilies, green
onions, lime juice, garlic, cilantro and
salt in a medium bowl. Toss together
to combine. Serve within 2 hours.

Spicy Raspberry
Salsa

Use this fruity salsa with fish, chicken or vegetables.

---

yields: 2 cups

2 cups raspberries
2 jalapeño chilies,
seeded & minced
2 tbsp red onion, minced
2 tbsp cilantro, minced
2 tbsp raspberry vinegar
¼ tsp salt

Place raspberries, chilies, red onion, cilantro, raspberry vinegar and salt in a medium bowl. Toss lightly to combine flavors. Chill 1 hour and store up to 2 days.

Strawberry
Salsa

yields: 2 cups

1 pint strawberries, diced
2 tbsp sugar
1 to 2 serrano chilies, minced
½ cup red onion, minced
3 tbsp raspberry vinegar
2 tbsp cilantro, minced
¼ tsp salt
¼ tsp freshly ground pepper

Place strawberries and sugar in a bowl. Cover and refrigerate for at least 1 hour. Add serrano chilies, red onion, vinegar and cilantro. Toss together lightly. Season with salt and pepper. Let salsa rest at room temperature for at least 20 minutes before serving.

Tomatillo
Salsa

---

suggested use

Tomatillos give this salsa a very refreshing taste, working well with fish and chicken dishes.

---

yields: 2½ cups

6 **medium** tomatillos
3 **medium** tomatoes, diced
½ **cup** red onion, minced
2 **cloves** garlic, minced
2 **to** 3 jalapeños,
seeded & minced
1 **tbsp** cilantro, minced
½ **tsp** ground cumin
½ **tsp** salt

Remove the husks from the tomatillos and dice. Place in a medium bowl with the tomatoes, red onion, garlic, chilies, cilantro, cumin and salt. Toss to combine. Use within 1 day.

55

Tropical
Salsa

---

suggested use

Try this salsa on grilled fish, especially salmon or mahi mahi.

---

yields: 2½ cups

½ *medium* pineapple, peeled,
cored *&* diced
4 *kiwis, peeled & diced*
1 *red or green* jalapeño,
seeded & minced
1 *tbsp* lemon juice
1 *tbsp* vegetable oil
1 *tbsp* basil, minced

Place pineapple, kiwi, chili, lemon juice and vegetable oil in a medium bowl. Toss to combine. Toss in basil. Let stand for 1 hour. Refrigerate up to 2 days.

Sauces

Generally a liquid, or semi liquid, sauces were, like chutneys and relishes, originally conceived to help mask the unpleasant tastes and smells of slightly spoiled foods. Today they are added to the finest of foods, often helping to bring out the delicious inherent flavors, and not mask them. With many of the spices used being rare and expensive, it is also believed that the ingredients in a sauce spoke for your financial status. We now have a wide variety of spices at our disposal, whether at the grocery store or specialty spice shops, and simple and exotic sauces have become a favorite staple in many people's meals.

In culinary arts, there are five basic sauces, referred to as the "mother sauces." They are béchamel, hollandaise (or mayonnaise), velouté (or sauce blonde), tomato, and espagnole sauce (or brown/ brune sauce). Mastering these five basic sauces will give you endless possibilities in your sauce creations and meals.

Some people still think of sauces as something to make dry meats edible, but as this book has also aimed to share the wonders of sous vide cooking with the revolutionary AquaChef, your sauces will never need to hide a dry or tough meat again.

So we now present what may be your most frequented portion of this book; after tasting these recipes, you will be hard pressed to find a meal that wouldn't be bettered by such exciting and flavorful sauces.

Apricot

Sauce

---

suggested use

*This sauce works well as a dipping sauce
with chicken or shrimp, or for basting.*

---

yields: 3 cups

¼ *cup* brown sugar
2½ *cups* apricot nectar
¼ *cup* tomato paste
3 *tbsp* Dijon mustard
2 *tsp* orange zest

In a medium saucepan, combine the brown sugar, apricot nectar, tomato paste, mustard and orange zest. Bring to a boil, stirring often and cook until thickened and bubbly. Cool before using for basting. Serve hot for dipping.

Béarnaise
Sauce

---

suggested use

This sauce works well with meat, fish, eggs, and vegetables.

---

yields: 1½ cups

8 tbsp unsalted butter
4 shallots, finely chopped
2 tbsp tarragon leaves
4 white peppercorns, crushed
¼ cup white wine vinegar
⅓ cup dry white wine
4 large egg yolks
¼ tsp salt
pinch cayenne pepper

Melt butter in a medium saucepan over medium heat. Do not over heat. Boil shallots, tarragon, and peppercorns in vinegar and wine in a medium saucepan (nonreactive) over medium heat until reduced to about 1/4 cup. Strain into top of double boiler. Whisk in egg yolks. Place over simmering water. Whisk constantly. When yolk mixture begins to thicken slightly, remove from heat and whisk in the melted butter very slowly. Whisk in the salt and cayenne. Add salt/cayenne as needed.

Béchamel

Sauce

suggested use

This sauce is delicious over broccoli or in a lasagna. For a thinner sauce, use 1 tbsp of butter to 1 tbsp flour. For thicker, 3-4 tbsp butter to 3-4 tbsp flour.

yields: 1 cup

2 tbsp butter
2 tbsp flour
½ tsp salt
⅛ tsp pepper
1 cup milk, warm

Melt butter in a saucepan over low heat. Blend in flour, salt, and pepper. Cook over low heat, stirring until it is mixed smooth and bubbling lightly. At this point you have a white roux. Remove the roux from heat. Stir in warm milk and whisk until roux is smooth and lump-free. Return to heat. Bring to a boil, stirring constantly. Boil for at least one minute.

Cajun Butter
Sauce

This sauce is great over tuna steaks or other meaty fish fillets. It also works well over chicken breasts.

yields: 1½ cups

½ *cup unsalted butter*
1 *tbsp dry vermouth*
1 *tbsp orange juice*
1 *tbsp orange zest*
2 *cloves garlic, minced*
1 *tsp Worcestershire sauce*
2 *tbsp paprika*
1 *tbsp garlic powder*
2 *tsp dried thyme*
½ *tsp dried oregano*
1 *tsp cayenne pepper*
1 *tsp salt*
1 *tsp freshly ground pepper*
½ *tsp hot pepper sauce*

Melt butter in a medium saucepan. Add in the remaining ingredients. Whisk to combine well and cook until just heated through.

Cilantro Chili
Sauce

---

suggested use

This spicy sauce works well with Southwestern fish or chicken.

---

yields: ½ cup

2 jalapeños, *finely chopped*
½ cup dry white wine
2 green onions, *chopped*
1 *tbsp* lime juice
1 *packed cup* cilantro
½ cup butter, melted & hot

Place chilies, wine, green onion and lime juice in a small saucepan. Bring to a boil and continue to cook until mixture is reduced by half. Cool about 5 minutes. Transfer chili mixture to a food processor or blender and puree. Add the cilantro and finely chop. With the machine running, add the hot melted butter. Serve immediately.

Cilantro Mint

Sauce

---

suggested use

This fresh sauce is great for lamb kabobs or lamb chops.

---

yields: 1½ cups

1½ *cups cilantro*
1 *cup mint*
5 *tbsp water*
1½ *tbsp white wine vinegar*
2 *tsp sugar*
1 *tsp curry powder*
1 *clove garlic, minced*
¼ *tsp red pepper flakes, crushed*

Place cilantro and mint in the food processor. Pulse to chop. Add water, vinegar, sugar, curry powder, garlic and red pepper flakes. Process until finely minced.

Citus Spice

---

suggested use

This spicy sweet sauce is great with ribs. It also works well with chicken wings or skewered shrimp.

---

yields: 1 cup

2 *tsp* orange zest
1 *cup* orange juice
2 *tbsp* lemon juice
2 *tbsp* sugar
2 *tsp* prepared horseradish
1 *tsp* ginger, minced

Place all ingredients in a blender or food processor and puree. Store in the refrigerator for up to 1 week.

Cranberry Orange

Sauce

---

suggested use

*This sauce is perfect for roast chicken or turkey.
It also works well over sliced roast pork.*

---

yields: ½ cup

2 *cups* cranberry juice
¼ *cup* brown sugar
¼ *cup* cider vinegar
1 *tsp* orange zest

Place cranberry juice in a 2-quart saucepan. Bring to a boil then cook down until reduced to 1 cup. Add brown sugar and vinegar and boil until mixture is syrupy and reduced to about ½ cup. Stir in zest and keep warm.

Creole

Sauce

suggested use

This sauce uses tomato sauce, which is one of the "Mother Sauces" and tastes great with fish. Also try it with the Spicy Turkey Breast AquaChef recipe on page 100.

yields: 4 cups

4 cups tomato sauce (page 90)
¾ cup onions, chopped
¾ cup celery, chopped
½ cup green pepper, diced
1 clove garlic, minced
1 bay leaf
½ tsp dried oregano
1 lemon's zest
to taste kosher salt
to taste black pepper, freshly ground
to taste cayenne pepper

In a heavy-bottomed saucepan, sauté the onions, green pepper, celery and garlic for about 5 minutes, or until the onions are translucent. Add the tomato sauce, bay leaf, oregano and lemon zest. Bring to a simmer and cook for about 15 minutes. Remove bay leaf, season with the salt, pepper and cayenne to taste.

Demi-Glace
Sauce

---

suggested use

A rich brown sauce, this is often used in French cuisine by itself or as a base for other sauces.

---

yields: 4 cups

Equal parts:
Espagnole Sauce (page 70)
beef stock

In a heavy-bottomed pot, combine equal parts Espagnole Sauce and beef stock, and reduce by half.

Strain through a fine sieve.

Espagnole
Sauce

---

suggested use

A French sauce with various explanations of where the name came from, it's perfect on a winter meat dish, or thick noodles.

---

yields: 1 quart

Mirepoix:
4 oz onions, *chopped*
2 oz celery, *chopped*
2 oz carrots, *chopped*

2 oz *butter*
2 oz *flour*
2 oz *tomato purée*

Bouquet Garni:
½ *bay leaf*
2-3 sprigs *fresh thyme*
2-3 sprigs *parsley*

½-2 qts *beef stock*

Roast the mirepoix over medium heat in the bottom of a heavy bottom sauce pot with the butter, until it turns a nice golden brown. Add in tomato purée and continue roasting for 2-3 minutes. Sprinkle in flour, and cook until the flour is well incorporated, about 5 minutes. Add beef stock and bouquet garni. Bring to a simmer, and gently simmer for about 2 hours, reducing the entire sauce down to 1qt. If too much evaporates during the cooking process, add more beef stock. Skim sauce as needed. Once sauce is finished cooking, pass it through a fine sieve until it reaches a smooth, consistent texture.

Garlic Ginger

---

suggested use

Try this sauce with chicken or shrimp.

---

yields: ½ cup

¼ cup onion, chopped
2 cloves garlic, minced
1 tbsp ginger, minced
2 tbsp lemon juice
¼ cup soy sauce
¼ tsp sugar
¼ tsp white vinegar

Place all ingredients in a blender or food processor and puree. Serve at room temperature. Keep covered in the refrigerator for 1 week.

Hollandaise
Sauce

This sauce is perfect for roast chicken or turkey.
It also works well over sliced roast pork.

yields: 3 cups

4 tbsp water
1 tbsp white wine vinegar
1 tbsp peppercorns, crushed
4 egg yolks
1 cup unsalted butter, melted
1 tbsp lemon juice
to taste salt

In a small pan over low heat, bring the water, vinegar, and peppercorns to a simmer. Continue for about 2-3 minutes, or until mixture reduces about a third. Strain the reduction into a stainless steel or glass bowl to cool.

Place the bowl over a pan of just-simmering water; add the egg yolks and stir until the mixture is lemon colored, thickened, and smooth. Do not allow the mixture's temperature to rise above room temperature or the eggs will coagulate. Let the melted butter cool and slowly pour into the mixture, stirring constantly until the sauce becomes thick and fluffy. Stir in the lemon juice and salt and continue to mix until sauce drips in a smooth ribbon from the whisk. Keep warm until served.

Honey Orange

---

suggested use

Use this to baste ham or with pork chops.

---

yields: 1 cup

½ cup honey
1 cup orange juice
½ tsp orange zest
¼ tsp dry mustard

Place honey, orange juice and zest, and mustard in a small saucepan. Simmer over a low heat until reduced slightly.

Lemon Sage

---

suggested use

This butter sauce is great with shrimp and scallops or any other seafood.

---

yields: ½ cup

½ *cup unsalted butter*
1 *tbsp lemon juice*
1 *tsp dried sage*
1 *tsp lemon zest*
½ *tsp salt*

Melt butter slowly in a small saucepan over low heat. Whisk in the lemon juice and zest, sage, and salt.

Mayonnaise

---

suggested use

*Use this anywhere you would use store-bought mayonnaise.
Try spicing it up by adding other ingredients at the end, such as
mustard, or horseradish.*

---

yields: 1 cup

1 egg yolk
2 tsp *sea salt*
2 tbsp *cider vinegar*
¼ cup *grapeseed oil*
¾ cup *extra virgin olive oil*

This recipe can be made with an immersion blender, food processor, or by mixing with a whisk by hand, but be extra careful to ensure the oil emulsifies, as stated in the instructions below. All steps should be using the blender, processor or whisk.

Mix together egg yolk, sea salt and cider vinegar until smooth and light in color. Extremely slowly, start mixing in the oil, drop by drop - you will see the mixture begin to emulsify. Continue adding the oil very slowly until the mixture thickens and is no longer liquid. Once it has become thicker and is clearly emulsifying, you can begin to add the oil a bit more quickly.

Mushroom
Sauce

A variation of the Velouté sauce, this mushroon sauce works with roasted or grilled meat dishes.

yields: 2 cups

1 *tbsp butter*
1 *cup mushrooms, sliced*
1 *shallot, chopped*
2 *tbsp sherry*
2 *cups demi-glace (page 69)*
to taste lemon juice

Heat the butter over medium heat in a heavy-bottomed saucepan, until it's frothy. Add the mushrooms and shallots and sauté for about 5 minutes until the mushrooms are soft and the shallots are translucent. Add the demi-glace, and bring to a boil, then lower the heat to a simmer, reducing the mixture for about 10 minutes. Stir in the sherry, and season to taste with the lemon juice. Serve immediately.

Mustard Dill

Sauce

---

suggested use

These flavors work well as a dipping or top sauce with shrimp or salmon, and other fish fillets, as well as with vegetables like asparagus.

---

yields: 1 cup

4 *tsp sugar*
1 *cup dill, minced*
1 *cup coarse-grained mustard*
¼ *cup white wine vinegar*
½ *cup mayonnaise (page 74)*
2 *tbsp olive oil*

Place sugar, dill, mustard, vinegar and mayonnaise in a blender or food processor. Blend until smooth. With machine still running add the oil, drop by drop until absorbed. Store covered in refrigerator up to one week.

Peppercorn

suggested use

This classic peppercorn sauce is delicious on a tri-tip steak.

yields: 1 cup

1 tbsp olive oil
1 shallot, minced
2 tsp black pepper,
freshly ground
1 cup heavy cream
to taste salt

Using the 1 tbsp of olive oil, coat a pan or skillet at medium heat. Add the shallots, and sauté until translucent. Add the freshly ground black pepper to your sautéed shallots and mix. Next add the 1 cup of heavy cream and mix. Let the sauce cook for a minute to thicken slightly. Add salt to taste.

Port Wine

Sauce

---

suggested use

A variation on the Espagnole sauce, this sauce works wonderfully with roast beef and steaks.

---

yields: 2 cups

2 *cups demi-glace*
4 *tbsp dry port wine*
1 *tbsp butter*

In a heavy-bottomed saucepan, heat the demi-glace to a simmer and reduce for about 10 minutes. Stir in the port wine and swirl in the butter. Serve right away.

Poblano Chili

Sauce

---

suggested use

*Spoon this sauce onto serving plates and top
with a cooked steak, chicken breasts or shrimp.*

---

yields: 1 cup

*2 poblano chilies,
roasted & peeled*
1 jalapeño, seeded & minced
½ cup red onion, chopped
2 cloves garlic, peeled
½ cup cilantro, chopped
¼ cup lime juice
2 tbsp water
2 tbsp olive oil
1 tsp salt

Place all ingredients in a food
processor or blender and puree until
a chunky paste is formed.

Provençale
Sauce

---

suggested use

*This delicious sauce is amazing with most
meats and fish.*

---

yields: 2 cups

2 cups tomato sauce (page 90)
½ onion, finely chopped
1 cup *tomatoes,*
peeled, seeded & chopped
1 clove *garlic, minced*
1 tsp Herbes de Provence
1 tbsp capers
1 tbsp *black olives, chopped*
to taste *kosher salt*
to taste *black pepper,*
freshly ground

In a heavy-bottomed saucepan, sauté the onions for about 5 minutes, or until they are translucent. Add the tomatoes, garlic and Herbes de Provençe. Continue to sauté for about 10 minutes, until the tomatoes are soft. Add the tomato sauce, capers and olives. Bring to a simmer and reduce for about 10 minutes. Season with the salt and pepper to taste.

Robert

Sauce

---

suggested use

This sauce, derived from the Espagnole sauce, works especially well with grilled pork, or other meats.

---

yields: 1¼ cup

1 tbsp butter
½ cup onion, finely minced
¼ cup white wine
1 tsp dry mustard
2 cups demi-glace

Melt the butter in a saucepan over medium heat. Add the onions and sauté for 1 minute. Add the wine and bring to a boil. Cook for about 2 minutes. Stir in the mustard. Add the demi-glace and reduce to medium heat. Simmer for 20 minutes. Remove from heat and serve.

Sesame Ginger
Sauce

suggested use

This sauce is great served warm with Asian food like spring rolls or dumplings, but would also work well with grilled chicken and pork.

yields: 3 cups

¼ *cup* soy sauce
½ *tsp* toasted sesame oil
1 *clove* garlic, minced
1 *tsp* green onions, chopped
1 *tbsp* water
2 *tbsp* hoisin sauce
¼ *tsp* ginger, minced
½ *tsp* sugar

Combine the soy sauce, sesame oil, garlic, green onions, water, hoisin sauce, ginger, and sugar in a small bowl and mix well. Add additional hoisin sauce to thicken mixture to your desired consistency if needed. Cover the sauce, and refrigerate for 1 to 2 hours to allow flavors to blend.

Spiced Lime

Sauce

---

suggested use

*This tangy spicy sauce is great with Asian
meat dishes.*

---

yields: 1 cup

6 *tbsp lime juice*
3 *tbsp fish sauce*
¼ *cup sugar*
½ *cup warm water*
1 *clove garlic, minced*
2 *serrano chilies,
finely chopped*

Combine all the ingredients in a
large bowl and mix until the sugar is
dissolved. Let sit for 30 minutes for
flavors to blend. Keep covered in the
refrigerator for up to 1 week.

Spicy Apricot

Sauce

---

suggested use

This chunky, spicy-sweet sauce is great over any sweet spice rub on pork, chicken or turkey.

---

yields: 1½ cups

3 jalapeños
10 oz dried apricots, chopped
¾ cup bourbon
¼ cup Dijon mustard
½ tsp cumin, ground
¼ tsp red pepper flakes, crushed
2 tbsp lime juice

Place chilies under the broiler, turning until blackened on all sides. Place in a paper bag to cool. Peel chilies and chop. Combine apricots, bourbon, mustard and cumin in a 2-quart saucepan. Bring to a boil and then simmer, uncovered, for 30 minutes. Transfer to a blender and puree. Stir in chopped chilies, red pepper flakes and lime juice.

Spicy Pineapple

Sauce

---

suggested use

This sweet and sour sauce is delicious over any type of citrus marinated fish or chicken, as well as pork.

---

yields: 2 cups

1 cup pineapple, chopped
2 cups pineapple juice
½ cup white wine vinegar
½ cup golden brown sugar
1 jalapeño, seeded & diced

Place the pineapple and pineapple juice in a large saucepan. Add the vinegar, brown sugar and jalapeño. Bring to a simmer and continue cooking until liquid is reduced by half.

Sweet Nut
Sauce

---

suggested use

Traditionally used as a dipping sauce for pork, beef or chicken satay. It also works well with roasted chicken.

---

yields: 1½ cups

½ cup crunchy peanut butter
1½ cups canned coconut milk,
unsweetened
¼ cup lemon juice
2 tbsp soy sauce
2 tbsp golden brown sugar
1 tsp ginger, minced
4 cloves garlic, minced
1 pinch cayenne pepper
¼ cup or more chicken stock
or water

Place peanut butter, coconut milk, lemon juice, soy sauce, brown sugar, ginger, garlic and cayenne in a saucepan. Cook, stirring constantly, over medium heat, until the sauce is thick and fairly smooth, about 10 minutes. Pour sauce into the blender and puree, adding the chicken stock to thin as necessary. Return to pan and heat until warm. Let cool.

Sweet & Spicy

Sauce

---

suggested use

Traditionally served with an asian BBQ chicken. It is also delicious with fried appetizers, like egg rolls.

---

yields: 1 cup

1 *cup* granulated sugar
½ *cup* water
½ *cup* white distilled vinegar
½ *tsp* salt
2 *tsp* Thai chili paste
(or add more to taste)

Place sugar, water, vinegar and salt in a small saucepan. Bring to a boil, stirring until sugar dissolves. Reduce heat and simmer until sauce is syrupy, but do not allow sauce to caramelize. About 15 minutes. Remove from heat and stir in the chili paste. Cool and refrigerate up to 5 days.

Thai Orange *Sauce*

---

suggested use

Serve this sauce over chicken or shrimp that has been cooked with Thai Curry or another spicy rub.

---

yields: 1 cup

3 *cloves garlic, minced*
1 *tbsp ginger, minced*
2 *serrano chilies, minced*
½ *tsp orange zest*
½ *cup orange juice*
¼ *cup dry sherry*
2 *tbsp fish sauce*
1 *tbsp cornstarch*
1 *tbsp vegetable oil*
2 *tbsp mint, chopped*
2 *tbsp cilantro, chopped*

Toss garlic, ginger and chilies in a small bowl. Stir together orange zest, orange juice, sherry, fish sauce and cornstarch in another small bowl. Heat oil in a medium skillet over medium heat. Cook the garlic mixture for 2 minutes, stirring constantly. Add the orange juice mixture and bring to a boil, stirring constantly. Stir in the mint and cilantro.

Thai Red Curry

Sauce

---

suggested use

Pour this over cooked chicken, pork or shrimp. It is also very good over grilled fish fillets.

---

yields: 1½ cups

1 *tbsp vegetable oil*
2 *tbsp* Thai *curry*
1 14 *oz* **can** *coconut milk,*
unsweetened
2 *tbsp* fish *sauce*
1 *tbsp brown sugar*
½ *tsp salt*
2 *tbsp cilantro, minced*

Heat oil in a medium saucepan. Add Thai curry and stir with the oil over medium low heat. Add the coconut milk and bring to a simmer. Stir in the fish sauce, sugar and salt. Taste for seasoning and stir in the cilantro just before serving.

Tomato
Sauce

*This classic sauce can be used with any number of
dishes, as well as added to other sauces found in this
book. It also tastes great with pasta.*

yields: 4 cups

2 tbsp extra virgin olive oil
1 medium onion, diced
4 cloves garlic, crushed
& sliced
1 cup basil, diced
½ cup red wine
1 tbsp sugar
to taste salt & black pepper,
freshly ground
1 28 oz can crushed or diced
tomatoes
1 tsp lemon juice
3 tbsp brandy

Put olive oil in medium sauce pan
over medium heat. Add garlic, basil,
onions, and spices. When onions
are translucent add the remainging
ingredients and bring to a boil.
Simmer for 45 minutes. Salt and
pepper to taste.

Tomato Ketchup
Sauce

---

suggested use

*Use this ketchup anywhere you would use
store-bought ketchup.*

---

yields: 10 cups

10 *lbs* tomatoes, *very ripe*
1 *red bell pepper, seeded
& chopped*
4 *large* onions, *chopped*
1½ *cups* cider vinegar
2 *cloves* garlic, *crushed*
1 *tsp* peppercorns
1 *tsp* whole allspice
1 *tsp* whole cloves
5 *cinnamon sticks*
1 *tsp* celery seed
½ *tsp* dry mustard
¼ *tsp* cayenne
4 *tbsp* brown sugar,
packed firmly
3 *tbsp* granulated sugar
1 *tsp* salt

Cut tomatoes into large chunks and puree in a food processor. Run through a coarse sieve to remove seeds and skins. Puree onions and bell pepper and add to strained tomato mixture. Cook this mixture over low heat until reduced by 1/3 to 1/2 and is much thicker.

Simmer all spices over low heat in the vinegar for 1/2 hour, remove from heat and allow to steep. Strain half of this mixture into thickened tomato mixture and stir. Stir. Add sugar, mustard, cayenne, and salt.

Taste the mixture and add more of the spicy vinegar if it seems to be needed. More sugar, mustard, salt, and cayenne can also be added to taste. The mixture can also be cooked longer to thicken to the desired consistency.

Velouté

Sauce

---

suggested use

Pour this over chicken, veal, or fish.

---

yields: 1 cup

2 *cups chicken or fish stock*
3 *tbsp butter*
3 *tbsp flour*
⅛ *tsp salt*
⅛ *tsp ground white pepper*

Bring stock to a boil and set aside. Melt butter in a 2-quart saucepan over low heat. Create a roux by whisking in the flour. Cook over medium heat, stirring continually, for 2-3 minutes, or until the roux is bubbly and begins to darken slightly. Remove from heat. Whisk in the stock until smooth. Return to medium heat and bring to a boil, whisking continuously. Reduce heat and simmer uncovered until sauce begins to thicken. Season with salt and pepper to taste. Serve fresh and warm.

Sous Vide Suggestions

Here you will find a few of our favorite sous vide recipes that we think work wonderfully with some of the chutneys, relishes, salsas, and sauces that have been featured so far in this book.

By no means is this a comprehensive list, as every recipe throughout can be used in any number of recipes, combined with your favorite sous vide AquaChef dishes to make delicious complete meals. We encourage you to experiment with different combinations, but to help give you some ideas, the recipes listed in this chapter are sure to impress and inspire.

AquaChef Eggs

with *Hollandaise Sauce*

yields: 1-2 servings

1 to 2 large eggs
(Hollandaise sauce on page 71)

Remove the basket from your AquaChef and set it aside. Fill the AquaChef with approximately 3.5 liters of water, and turn it on. Set the temperature to 146°F for a soft-cooked egg, or 160°F for a hard-cooked egg, and press the start button to preheat the water. The water will be preheated when the Indicator light changes from red to blue.

Make sure your eggs are clean and have no cracks. For this recipe you will not need to vacuum pack the eggs. Once the AquaChef is preheated, set the cook time to 45 minutes. Then place the eggs in the cooking basket and place it carefully into the AquaChef and put the lid on. Once the time is up the, AquaChef will beep. Carefully remove the basket from the AquaChef, as it will be hot. Remove the eggs from the basket and peel off the shell. Serve over toast with the Hollandaise sauce on top.

Cajun Halibut

with *Spicy Mango Chutney*

yields: 2 servings

8-12 oz fresh halibut
to taste salt
1 tsp cajun seasoning
½ tsp chili powder

Set up AquaChef by filling the water basin with water to the max fill line and turn on the the AquaChef to preheat to 135°F.

Divide the halibut into two serving portions. Season with salt, cajun seasoning and chili powder. Lightly rub the seasoning into the halibut. Place each portion into a Seal 'n Fresh Bag and seal using the Seal 'n Fresh Vacuum Sealer. Place the halibut into a preheated AquaChef, and set the timer for 30 minutes

Once the time is up the, AquaChef will beep. Carefully remove the basket from the AquaChef, as it will be hot. Carefully remove the halibut from the bag and serve with the Spicy Mango Chutney found on page 36.

Lobster Tail

 *with* Lemon Sage Sauce

---

yields: 1-2 servings

1 to 2 large lobster tails
to taste salt
(Lemon Sage sauce on page 73)

Remove the basket from your AquaChef and set it aside. Fill the AquaChef with approximately 3.5 liters of water. Plug it in and turn it on. Set the temperature to 140° F and press the start button to preheat the water. The water will be preheated when the Indicator light changes from red to blue.

Sprinkle the lobster tails with salt, and place into a Seal 'n Fresh vacuum-sealed bag. Seal the bag and vacuum out as much air as possible. Once the AquaChef is preheated, set the cook timer to 45 minutes. Then place the lobster in the cooking basket and place it carefully into the AquaChef and put the lid on.

When the time is up the AquaChef will beep. Carefully remove the basket from the AquaChef, as it will be hot. Remove the lobster from the bag, and place on serving plates. Pour the Lemon Sage sauce on top and serve.

Salmon

with *Avocado* *Salsa*

---

yields: 1-2 servings

1 - 1¼ lbs filet of salmon
1 lemon
to taste salt & pepper

Remove the basket from your AquaChef and set it aside. Fill the AquaChef with approximately 3.5 liters of water. Plug it in and turn it on. Set the temperature to 126° F and press the start button to preheat the water. The water will be preheated when the Indicator light changes from red to blue.

Slice the lemon into ¼ inch slices. Salt and pepper the salmon to taste on both sides. Arrange the lemon slices on the flesh side of the filet and place them into a Seal 'n Fresh vacuum-sealed bag. Seal the bag and vacuum out as much air as possible.

Once the AquaChef is preheated, set the cook time to 45 minutes, and place the salmon in the cooking basket into the AquaChef and put the lid on. Once the time is up, the AquaChef will beep. Carefully remove the basket from the AquaChef, it will be hot. Remove the salmon from the bag and serve immediately with the Avocado Salsa from page 44.

Spicy Turkey Breast

with *Creole Sauce*

yields: 1-2 servings

1 turkey breast 1 tsp salt
2 tsp chili powder ½ tsp pepper
1 tsp cumin (Creole sauce on page 68)

Remove the basket from your AquaChef, fill the AquaChef with 3.5 liters of water, and turn it on. Set the temperature to 146° F and press the start button to preheat the water. The water will be preheated when the Indicator light changes from red to blue.

Sprinkle the turkey breast with chili powder, cumin, salt and pepper. Place in a Seal 'n Fresh bag and vacuum out as much air as possible. Once the AquaChef is preheated, set the cook time to 1 hour. Then place the turkey breast in the cooking basket and place it carefully into the AquaChef and put the lid on.

Once the time is up, the AquaChef will beep. Carefully remove the basket from the AquaChef, as it will be hot. Remove the turkey breasts from the bag and dry it lightly with a paper towel. Slice the breast and serve with the Creole Suace.

Tri-Tip Steak

with

Peppercorn

Sauce

yields: 1-2 servings

*1-1½" **thick** tri-tip steak*
to taste salt & pepper
(Peppercorn sauce on page 77)

Remove the basket from your AquaChef and set it aside. Fill the AquaChef with approximately 3.5 liters of water, and turn it on. Set the AquaChef's temperature to 134° F and press the start button to preheat the water. The water will be preheated when the Indicator light changes from red to blue.

Using the salt and pepper, season the meat to taste, and place in a Seal 'n Fresh bag and vacuum out as much air as possible. Once the AquaChef is preheated, set the cook time on your AquaChef to 1 hour. Place the tri-tip in the cooking basket and place it carefully into the AquaChef and put the lid on.

Once the time is up, the AquaChef will beep. Carefully remove the basket from the AquaChef, as it will be hot. Remove the tri-tip from the bag and dry lightly with a paper towel and place the tri-tip in the pan and sear each side for about 1 minute. Place the tri-tip on a plate, add the sauce as a topping, and serve.